Nathaniel Macon of North Carolina
Three Views of His Character and Creed

Drawing of Nathaniel Macon by Katie Price, 2007, based on the W. G. Randall drawing and the Rober D. Gauley portrait in the U.S. Capitol. Randall made his drawing after Macon's death (he refused many offer to do one while alive), relying on the descriptions of men who had known Macon.

Nathaniel Macon of North Carolina
Three Views of His Character and Creed

BY

WILLIAM S. PRICE JR.

North Carolina Office of Archives and History
Raleigh
2008

In association with the North Caroliniana Society
Chapel Hill

North Carolina Department of Cultural Resources
Lisbeth C. Evans, *Secretary*

Office of Archives and History
Jeffrey J. Crow, *Deputy Secretary*

Division of Historical Resources
David L. S. Brook, *Director*

Historical Publications Section
Donna E. Kelly, *Administrator*

———••◆••———

———••◆••———

Contents

———•◆━◆•———

Cover: "Courthouse Warrenton, 1812," painting by a Miss Somerville in the Warren County Memorial Library, Warrenton, North Carolina. A typed label on the back of the painting reads, "Presented to Warren County by B. S. Bronson, Jr. in memory of B. S. Bronson and Alice Sommerville Bronson." Manly Wade Wellman, who reproduced an image of the painting in his *The County of Warren, North Carolina, 1586-1917*, notes: "It is said the two figures in the left foreground represent Dr. James Brehon and William Falkener, the schoolmaster."

Foreword

————•◆◆•————

As I write these words, it is 2008—two hundred and fifty years since the birth of Nathaniel Macon, the only lifelong North Carolinian ever to have been Speaker of the U.S. House of Representatives and the first American to be elected to multiple consecutive terms as Speaker. Parts of his political legacy endure in his state and region and are evidenced in the stands of politicians as different as Jesse Helms and John Edwards. Today, few people comprehend Macon's persistent influence on the conservative/"populist" dynamic of his region, and this book seeks to suggest a fuller understanding of his legacy.

The community of Macon, North Carolina, was a special place for me from my earliest memories. My mother was born there in the Rodwell homeplace in 1905, and my brother, in 1933. My beloved aunt Ida and her husband, Marvin Drake, still lived in that house when I came along in 1941. Throughout the 1940s and 1950s, I visited her often, sometimes for a week or more during summertime. Named for Nathaniel Macon, the town had a railroad depot (my grandfather Rodwell had once been stationmaster there), a post office, four churches (two black, two white), a two-story hotel, a school, a tiny commercial district, and a small cluster of dwellings on either side of the Seaboard Air Line Railway tracks that divided the village. Farms were numerous in the surrounding countryside and pushed right up against the town. The homeplace of my distant cousin Nathaniel Macon Thornton had scores of acres with several outbuildings, including a stable where he kept horses. Mac (pronounced "make") allowed me to ride whenever I wanted—which was much of the time once I reached the age of nine or so. My favorite was a horse named Jimmy, which I rode mostly on my kinsman's ample fenced property. But in 1952, Mac let me take Jimmy off the place (accompanied on their own mounts by a man who worked for him and that man's young son) to travel to what was the only "historic site" in the area—Buck Spring plantation, the home of Warren County's then most famous native, Nathaniel Macon.

At the end of the three miles or so of dirt road that took us there, I saw an unimpressive frame house not much different from many dwellings still lived in throughout the county. If the house failed to impress—I had seen *Gone with the Wind*, and clearly Buck Spring was no Tara—one feature on the place riveted. A few hundred yards from the dwelling was a tiny cemetery with a mound of stones in it. It was the grave of Nathaniel Macon, and its marker mentioned that he had known Thomas Jefferson. Drawn to history already, I knew that Jefferson was a great man, and perhaps the man under the stones would be worth getting to know. Forrest Harris, the adult in our trio, said that Mr. Macon had asked that visitors add rocks to his grave, and we found some to toss on the pile. I promised myself that I would find out more about Nathaniel Macon some day.

Twenty-four years later, I remembered that promise when I heard Harry Watson, a young professor from the University of North Carolina at Chapel Hill, deliver a paper to the North Carolina Literary and Historical Association on antebellum politics in the state. There were a number of quotes from Nathaniel Macon in the piece, and Harry graciously shared those sources with me. I was far more familiar with the seventeenth and eighteenth centuries than the nineteenth, so the reading I needed to do to understand Macon's life and times more fully would have to wait. The demands of my job and a young family at home took precedence.

In 1995, I took early retirement from the North Carolina Division of Archives and History and began teaching at Meredith College in Raleigh, where I offered courses in various facets of southern and public history for eleven years. With long stretches of each summer free of teaching obligations, I began reading about Nathaniel Macon and his era. I dove into the rich archival and manuscript collections of the North Carolina State Archives, the University of North Carolina at Chapel Hill (UNC), and Duke University, assisted by the able staff members of these institutions. For printed sources I benefited from libraries at UNC (especially the remarkable North Carolina Collection), North Carolina State University, and Meredith College.

Having early on loved a town that was native to my mother, Elizabeth Rodwell Price, and my brother, Reynolds, within a county that also had produced my father, William Solomon Price, in nearby Warrenton in 1900; having many Rodwell and Price relatives still in the county, some dead, some living; and having seen Buck Spring at the instance of a man named for Macon, I had some real emotional incentives to keep working. Then in 1998, I read the autobiography of Macon's close political and personal friend, Martin Van Buren. On his opening page, Van Buren reveals that he had finally found the time to write a memoir late in life, buoyed by the invigorating environment of a beautiful Italian town on the Gulf of Naples, within sight of Vesuvius. As I read the name of the town, I laughed out loud. It was Sorrento, birthplace and home until she was fourteen of my wife of four decades, Pia Tavernise. Were the Fates prodding me to quit reading so much and begin writing?

In 2001, I published my first article on Macon in the *North Carolina Historical Review*. Although I had been invited to submit the piece elsewhere, I wanted it to be in the *Review*, not only because of that journal's distinguished record, but because it provided illustrations, and that first piece (featuring Macon's physical and cultural environment) needed instructive images. Three years later, the *Review* published my next article, focusing on Macon's political ideology. In the case of both articles, I had the benefit of working with the first-class staff of the Historical Publications Section of the Office of Archives and History, especially Donna Kelly and Anne Miller. The fact that this relationship has continued into the publication of the current work is a genuine pleasure for me.

Offered herein are the two earlier pieces, "Nathaniel Macon, Planter" and "Nathaniel Macon, Antifederalist," and a heretofore unpublished essay, "Thomas Jefferson and Nathaniel Macon: A Republican Friendship." They appear here in reverse chronological order; that is, the newest article appears first and the oldest, last. What I have tried to do in the three pieces is to illuminate Nathaniel Macon's character, motivations, and values as demonstrated in his life and career—his agrarianism, his beliefs, his personality, his milieu, his politics, and, above all, his steadfast devotion to what he believed to be the legacy of the American Revolution. There is inevitably some overlap of facts and ideas from one essay to another, as each article was designed to stand alone. However, I hope that all three complement one another sufficiently to offer them without excisions or additions for greater unity.

In the case of all three essays, I have benefited from the careful and critical readings of two exemplary historians (and even better friends), Jeffrey Crow and Don Higginbotham. Sometimes I did not heed their advice, but I was always informed by it. Other readers critiqued the two previously published pieces to their improvement. I acknowledge them in those articles and will not repeat their names. I am very grateful to have had the useful criticism of my former student, Elizabeth Crowder, in the new essay on the friendship with Jefferson. Again, I have not always heeded her counsel and so bear responsibility for my own words. I am likewise grateful to Barton College and the Wilson County Historical Society for offering me the BB&T Endowed Annual Lecture at the college in the fall of 2006. That commitment forced me to get to work on the final essay without the foot-dragging that my recent retirement from Meredith might have caused. The piece offered here is fuller than the one delivered at Barton and better for the experience (and good questions) I had there. Also, I am honored that the North Caroliniana Society has chosen to include this book among its distinguished imprints. The Society's secretary and general editor, H. G. Jones, is one of the premier public historians in the nation and gave me my start in the profession when he hired me to head the North Carolina Colonial Records Project in 1971. North Carolina is fortunate to have the Society doing so many worthy things to support the state's history and literature.

As my research progressed, I became increasingly intrigued by Macon's career and stature among his contemporaries. Most revealing to me was his persistent championing of self-sufficient farmers and laborers (all of them white). Some modern observers label proponents of the working classes "populists." A strong populist vein is still part of North Carolina politics among candidates of both major parties. While it is impossible to know how a nineteenth-century figure would vote two centuries later, I believe that Macon would have felt most comfortable with the twentieth-century Tar Heel politician W. Kerr Scott, governor and U.S. senator.

In closing, the emotional element of my work has been as compelling as any intellectual appeal. As stirring as my boyhood memories are, the larger pull has been the people I love most. I have already named my remembered parents, my brother, and my wife above. I complete the list with the names of my daughters, Marie Elizabeth Price Keelan and Katherine Reynolds Price McBrayer, and my grandchildren, Katherine Eileen Keelan and Imogene Price McBrayer. I hope that all of them will accept this offering as a reminder of a world that once was and a place that still is.

William S. Price Jr.

Thomas Jefferson and Nathaniel Macon: A Republican Friendship

———•◦•●•◦•———

Less than four months before his death, Thomas Jefferson wrote a letter for his grandson to hand deliver to Sen. Nathaniel Macon of North Carolina. The text of the message in the unsteady but legible hand of the great man reads:

> My grandson Th. Jefferson Randolph, the bearer of this letter on a journey to the North, will pass 2 or 3 days perhaps in Washington. I cannot permit him to do this without presenting him to a friend of so long standing, whom I consider as the strictest of our models of genuine republicanism. Let him be able to say when you are gone but not forgotten that he had seen Nathanl. Macon on whose tomb will be written Ultimus Romanorum [Last of the Romans]. I only ask you to give him a hearty shake of the hand on my acct. as well as his, assuring you that he merits it as a man & citizen to which I add my unceasing affection to yourself.[1]

Even when one concedes that Jefferson was a skilled politician given to occasional flattery, this brief letter surely testifies to his regard for Macon; nor is such a letter without precedent in the long friendship of the two men.[2]

Of the two, Jefferson is the better known, of course. His image is on our money, his face is on Rushmore, and on and on. He is an American icon. Were he remembered only as the president who managed the Louisiana Purchase, his fame would be assured. But his achievements are abundant on either side of his White House years.[3] Macon, as the less famous of the pair, deserves a brief overview to

---

1. Thomas Jefferson to Nathaniel Macon, March 24, 1826, Series 1, General Correspondence, 1651-1827, Thomas Jefferson Papers, American Memory, Library of Congress, Washington, D.C. http://memory.loc.gov/ammem/collections/jefferson_papers/mtjser1.html (accessed June 28, 2006). This collection will hereinafter be cited as Jefferson Papers. The transcription omits Jefferson's occasionally erratic punctuation, brings superscripts down to the line, and translates the Latin tribute in square brackets but is otherwise literal.

2. On Jefferson's political skills, see Bernard Bailyn, *To Begin the World Anew: The Genius and Ambiguities of the American Founders* (New York: Alfred A. Knopf, 2003), 45-46; and James Sterling Young, *The Washington Community, 1800-1828* (New York: Columbia University Press, 1966), 129-131, 168-170. Precedents include Thomas Jefferson to Nathaniel Macon, October 10, 1823, Jefferson Papers; Jefferson to Macon, August 19, 1821, in Paul Leicester Ford, ed., *The Writings of Thomas Jefferson*, 10 vols. (New York: G. P. Putnam's Sons, 1892-1899), 10:192-193; and Thomas Hart Benton, *Thirty Years' View . . . from 1820 to 1850* (1875; reprint, New York: George Braziller, 1963), 32.

3. The primary and secondary literature on Jefferson is immense. Two excellent single-volume introductions are Noble E. Cunningham Jr., *In Pursuit of Reason: The Life of Thomas Jefferson* (New York: Ballantine Books, 1988); and Joseph J. Ellis, *American Sphinx: The Character of Thomas Jefferson* (New York: Alfred A. Knopf, 1997). For a fuller rendering, see the magisterial six volumes by Dumas Malone, entitled *Jefferson and His Time*, completed in 1981; individual volumes in this series will be cited by their

highlight those points that most acutely intersected with Jefferson's career and legacy. Because a majority of those contacts involved politics, the following summary stresses Macon's political life.

Macon was the sixth of eight children born to Gideon Macon and Priscilla Jones, in what would eventually become Warren County, North Carolina. He was not yet four years old when his well-to-do father died, probably early in 1762. Priscilla sent at least two of her sons (Nathaniel was one of them) to Charles Pettigrew's school in nearby Bute County Courthouse in 1766, and Nathaniel headed to the College of New Jersey (later Princeton) in 1774 along with his older brother, John. Nathaniel was a member of the Class of 1778, but the coming of the American Revolution interrupted his studies in 1776, and he likely left the school for good when President John Witherspoon dismissed all students that November because of nearby warfare.[4]

Returning to North Carolina, Macon eventually settled in northern Warren County at the end of 1779, two weeks after his twenty-first birthday, on land willed to him by his father. Nathaniel named the plantation he built there Buck Spring; it would remain home until his death in 1837.

Macon's plantation was close to the Roanoke River and the prosperous nearby town of Halifax, and he came to know prominent planters like William Richardson Davie, who would become a Revolutionary War hero and later a leading Federalist, and Willie Jones, a friend and ally of Jefferson and later the leading opponent of the U.S. Constitution of 1787 in North Carolina. Nathaniel became a protégé of Jones, as did his brothers John and Harrison.[5]

Having served briefly in a New Jersey militia company in 1776, Macon joined a North Carolina unit in 1780 and a year later was elected to the state senate, where he served until 1786. He married Hannah Plummer in 1783. When she died seven years later, Macon ended his brief withdrawal from political service by accepting election to the U.S. House of Representatives in 1791. Rising steadily through the ranks, he began to attract the notice of James Madison and Jefferson, especially for his outspoken opposition to the Jay Treaty in 1796 and the Sedition Act in 1798.

---

unique titles below. There is also a first-rate Web site on Jefferson with splendid images, certain primary texts, and an excellent biographical sketch. See http://www.monticello.org.

4. The best source on Macon at Princeton and one of the two best biographical sketches of Macon available is Wesley Frank Craven, "Nathaniel Macon," in *Princetonians: A Biographical Dictionary*, volume 3: *1776-1783*, ed. Richard A. Harrison (Princeton, N.J.: Princeton University Press, 1981), 230-236. See also William S. Price Jr., "Nathaniel Macon, Planter," *North Carolina Historical Review* 78 (April 2001): 187-190. Macon likely studied under Pettigrew's classically based instruction for seven years. See William E. Dodd, *The Life of Nathaniel Macon* (Raleigh, N.C.: Edwards and Broughton, 1903), 4-6.

5. Price, "Nathaniel Macon, Planter," 191-194; Norman K. Risjord, *The Old Republicans: Southern Conservatism in the Age of Jefferson* (New York: Columbia University Press, 1965), 28-29; William S. Price Jr., "Nathaniel Macon, Antifederalist," *North Carolina Historical Review* 81 (July 2004): 293-296.

Nathaniel Macon was born in 1758 in what would eventually become Warren County. He settled in northern Warren County at the end of 1779, on land willed to him by his father. The plantation he built there, Buck Spring, was close to the Roanoke River and the prosperous town of Halifax. Macon remained at Buck Spring until his death in 1837. Photograph by William S. Price Jr., 1998.

They saw him as the leader of what would develop into the Democratic-Republican (called Republican) Party in North Carolina, which would ultimately put both Jefferson, then Madison into the White House.

A year after Jefferson's presidential win in 1800, Macon was elected Speaker of the House of Representatives. He would be re-elected twice more until 1807. After losing the speakership, Macon allied himself with a group of congressmen, variously called Tertium Quid or Old Republicans, who generally opposed any measures that expanded federal power at the expense of the states or increased executive power as against legislative. While Macon's close friend John Randolph of Roanoke was an Old Republican leader and an acerbic critic of his kinsman

Thomas Jefferson from 1806 on, Macon never attacked the presidency with the relish of some of his fellow Quids.

Macon chaired the Foreign Relations Committee of the House from 1809 to 1810 and remained a respected figure in the whole chamber. In 1815, he reluctantly left the lower house for the Senate, where he attained prominence. He chaired the Foreign Relations Committee from 1818 to 1826 and was President Pro Tempore from 1826 until his resignation from the Senate in 1828.

Back home in Buck Spring, Macon gratefully resumed the life of a planter and briefly returned to public service in the North Carolina Constitutional Convention of 1835 (where he was unanimously elected president), and in the national presidential contest of 1836 as an elector for his longtime friend Martin Van Buren. When he died the following year, he was mourned throughout his native state and the entire South.[6]

Both Jefferson and Macon were born and reared as British subjects at a time when loyalty to the Crown was assumed in the American colonies. They were nurtured in a society and culture grounded in certain British values, beliefs, and practices. To be sure, Americans early on modified and even rejected some Old World norms, but their basic concepts of law, civil rights, and politics were English. The British legacies of liberty and freedom from arbitrary government became touchstones of the growing American resistance to Crown policies after the end of the French and Indian War in 1763. That resistance would ultimately foster rebellion.[7] Jefferson reached manhood during the turbulent decade of the 1760s (he was twenty years old in 1763), and young Macon began his schooling with a master who drilled his pupils in Greek and Latin texts that portrayed virtuous men struggling to defend liberty against tyrants.[8]

By 1775, of course, armed combat between Britain and its American colonies had begun. For revolutionaries, the fight was essential to secure a future free of the

6. This summary relies heavily on the best modern biography of Macon, Stephen J. Barry, "Nathaniel Macon: The Prophet of Pure Republicanism, 1758-1837" (Ph.D. diss., State University of New York at Buffalo, 1995). For Clyde Wilson's excellent biographical sketch, see *Dictionary of North Carolina Biography*, s.v. "Macon, Nathaniel." Dodd's 1903 biography noted above is still quite useful but in need of updating, especially in light of Barry's research. In addition to the city of Macon, Georgia, and the town of Macon, North Carolina, there are counties named for Macon in Alabama, Georgia, Illinois, Missouri, North Carolina, and Tennessee.

7. Forrest McDonald, *Novus Ordo Seclorum: The Intellectual Origins of the Constitution* (Lawrence: University Press of Kansas, 1985), 76-78; Stanley Elkins and Eric McKitrick, *The Age of Federalism* (New York: Oxford University Press, 1993), 6-7; Gordon S. Wood, *The Creation of the American Republic, 1776-1787* (Chapel Hill: University of North Carolina Press, 1969), 48-53.

8. Carl J. Richard, *The Founders and the Classics: Greece, Rome, and the American Enlightenment* (Cambridge, Mass.: Harvard University Press, 1995), 7-13, 45; Elkins and McKitrick, *Age of Federalism*, 48; Price, "Nathaniel Macon, Planter," 188. Jefferson's admiration for classical Greece and Rome is most stunningly displayed in his plan for the University of Virginia and his lifelong enjoyment of the literature of antiquity. See Jefferson to Peter Carr, January 21, 1812, in Peter S. Onuf, ed., *Thomas Jefferson: An Anthology* (St. James, N.Y.: Brandywine Press, 1999), 220; and Jefferson to Macon, January 12, 1819, in Ford, ed., *Writings of Jefferson*, 10:120-121.

Like Macon, Thomas Jefferson supported a balanced government with a separation of powers between branches, and both men upheld the small-scale, landowning, independent yeoman as the model citizen in a government that honored individual merit. Jefferson applauded Macon's outspoken opposition to the Jay Treaty and the Sedition Act. Bust of Thomas Jefferson, 1789, by Jean-Antoine Houdon, reproduced courtesy of Monticello/Thomas Jefferson Foundation, Inc., Charlottesville, Virginia.

corruption and decay that they believed had infected the British monarchy.[9] From the late seventeenth century over the ensuing nine decades, colonists became increasingly experienced in governing themselves and in honing their own political practices. As they contended with Crown-appointed governors, American political leaders not only became skillful legislators but also forged their own

9. Lance Banning, *The Jeffersonian Persuasion: Evolution of a Party Ideology* (Ithaca, N.Y.: Cornell University Press, 1978), 81; Wood, *Creation of the American Republic*, 31-33; Robert Dawidoff, *The Education of John Randolph* (New York: W. W. Norton and Co., 1979), 150.

elected lower houses of assembly into effective instruments for asserting their notions of home rule. Many colonists resented a governor's ability to dismiss a legislature as conferring undue power on an executive. The Crown's prerogative to review and disallow legislation progressed from being a minor irritant in the 1690s to a major affront by the 1770s. Indeed, of the seventeen charges leveled against George III in the Declaration of Independence, eleven touched in some way on royal attempts to curtail provincial legislative authority.[10] For many colonials, the increasing use of appointive offices and other governmental favors by Sir Robert Walpole during the reign of George II and continued by Walpole's ministerial successors into the rule of George III portended a British dominance that fostered vice before virtue and corruption before honor. Patronage and borough-manipulation had subverted Parliament and Crown alike, and many Americans began to see themselves as the true guardians of England's Glorious Revolution of the 1680s.[11]

As committed revolutionaries, Jefferson and Macon distrusted British rule and believed that constitutional safeguards would deter American government from mimicking the most repressive features of the colonial system. They wanted balanced governments with a separation of powers between branches, no hereditary offices or titles, annual legislative elections, limits on patronage, and strict curbs on executive prerogative. Jefferson and Macon (and many other Revolutionary leaders) upheld a republican system of government promoting political (but not social) equality as ideal. The small-scale, landowning, independent yeoman was the model citizen in a government that valued individual merit over any accident of birth. Macon believed that all government was inherently corrupt and that the extent of corruption was proportional to the size of the government and its distance from the governed. The further removed elected officials were from their voters, the more liable they were to malevolent lawmaking. There was more potential danger from a national government than a state, and more from a state government than a county.[12]

The American Revolution was and remained a defining moment for Jefferson and Macon. Whether serving as principal author of the Declaration of Independence or as a soldier in the ranks, each man throughout his long life remained

10. Jack P. Greene, *The Quest for Power: The Lower Houses of Assembly in the Southern Royal Colonies, 1689-1776* (Chapel Hill: University of North Carolina Press, 1963), 438-453; John Richard Alden, *The American Revolution* (New York: Harper Torchbooks, 1962), 150-163.

11. Banning, *Jeffersonian Persuasion*, 73-75, 126; Wood, *Creation of the American Republic*, 57-58, 78-79; Dumas Malone, *Jefferson and the Ordeal of Liberty* (Boston: Little, Brown and Co., 1962), 265-266.

12. McDonald, *Novus Ordo Seclorum*, 78; Wood, *Creation of the American Republic*, 48-53; Harry L. Watson, *Liberty and Power: The Politics of Jacksonian America* (New York: Noonday Press, 1990), 6, 43-46; Sean Wilentz, *The Rise of American Democracy: Jefferson to Lincoln* (New York: W. W. Norton and Co., 2005), 15-17, 36; Barry, "Nathaniel Macon," 170-171.

Anglophobic and remembered the ordeal of 1776 as a glorious time when freedom overthrew tyranny.[13]

After the fighting ended, neither Jefferson nor Macon participated in the national constitution-making that ensued. Jefferson was in France as U.S. minister from 1785 to 1789, although he maintained an active correspondence with James Madison and others on constitutional matters, and Macon had withdrawn from politics after 1785 to develop his plantation and help to raise his young family. Macon's brother John was at the Hillsborough Convention of 1788 (chaired by Willie Jones), and the siblings surely would have discussed pertinent issues both before and after that body declined to ratify. Neither Jefferson nor Macon was enthusiastic about the Constitution of 1787.[14]

When Washington was installed as president of the United States in 1789, the Revolution's greatest hero asked Jefferson to join his cabinet as secretary of state; he did so early in 1790. Soon, he would confront his most formidable foe, Alexander Hamilton, secretary of the treasury. Hamilton was Jefferson's equal intellectually and his opposite in matters of federal consolidation, constitutional interpretation, economic programs, and policy toward England and France, positions that inevitably led to the formation of divergent political parties. It was in this pregnant atmosphere that Nathaniel Macon entered Congress in 1791.[15] As Hamilton began to carry the day on such paramount issues as the assumption of state debts, creation of a national bank, encouragement of commerce and manufacturing, and a more conciliatory policy toward England (as France spiraled downward toward the blood-soaked Terror), Jefferson became increasingly alarmed, as did his fellow Virginian James Madison. Jefferson was profoundly worried that Washington—whom both Hamilton and Jefferson saw as a father figure—increasingly supported Hamilton's positions. As 1793 closed, Jefferson resigned from the cabinet in mounting frustration.[16]

---

13. Malone, *Jefferson and the Ordeal of Liberty*, 265-266; Price, "Nathaniel Macon, Antifederalist," 293-294; Elkins and McKitrick, *Age of Federalism*, 209-210; Ellis, *American Sphinx*, 125. Among Jefferson's many anti-British statements, one of the most striking is in a letter to the Marquis de Lafayette of June 16, 1792, in Onuf, ed., *Jefferson: An Anthology*, 138-139; among Macon's many anti-British statements, one of the clearest is in *Register of Debates*, 19th Cong., 1st sess., 695-696. It is likewise instructive to read Jefferson's original draft of the Declaration of Independence—before Congress tempered much of its defiance—in Onuf, ed., *Jefferson: An Anthology*, 42-45.

14. Banning, *Jeffersonian Persuasion*, 114n; Bailyn, *To Begin the World Anew*, 53-54; Price, "Nathaniel Macon, Antifederalist," 294-295. Jefferson expressed his lingering concerns about the federal constitution near the end of his life in 1821: "It is not by consolidation, or concentration of powers, but by their distribution, that good government is effected. . . . Were we directed from Washington when to sow, & when to reap, we should want bread." See Onuf, ed., *Jefferson: An Anthology*, 125.

15. There is abundant literature on the Jefferson/Hamilton struggles. The best starting point is Elkins and McKitrick, *Age of Federalism*, 223-244, 257-263.

16. Elkins and McKitrick, *Age of Federalism*, 211, 284-292; Don Higginbotham, *Revolution in America: Considerations and Comparisons* (Charlottesville: University of Virginia Press, 2005), 42; Don Higginbotham, *George Washington: Uniting a Nation* (Lanham, Md.: Rowman and Littlefield Publishers, 2002), 66, 82-83.

He communicated regularly with an alarmed Madison in Congress and, freed from his official duties, sharpened his arguments against the centralizing policies of Hamilton and Washington. This period saw the growth of Democratic-Republican societies throughout the country, the widespread opposition to the federal excise tax on whiskey that generated the short-lived Whiskey Rebellion, and a widening divide between Hamiltonian warmth toward England and Jeffersonian predilection for France. Though many Americans, like George Washington, despised the notion of political parties, they were compelled to choose sides—with Hamilton and the Federalists or with Jefferson and the Republicans. Macon chose the latter. With the election of John Adams as president in 1796 and Washington's retirement to Mount Vernon, party divisions were out in the open.[17]

During the 1790s, the establishment of distinctly Federalist and Republican newspapers heightened partisanship. The two most influential journals were based in Philadelphia. John Fenno's *Gazette of the United States* was pro-Federalist, and Philip Freneau's *National Gazette*, pro-Republican. Both offered strong editorial opinions, and Fenno sometimes printed Alexander Hamilton's pieces under a pseudonym, as was the customary practice. Freneau likewise offered space for James Madison and other friends of Jefferson to air their views. Wrapped in his lifelong aversion to open confrontation, Jefferson frequently fed ideas to Madison or James Monroe but did not assume a pen name himself. Madison had recruited Freneau, and Jefferson had given him a minor post in the State Department, so there was little doubt about who was supporting the *National Gazette*, just as there was little mystery about Hamilton's role in Fenno's paper.[18] Having experienced the "newspaper war" of 1792 and beyond as a young congressman, Nathaniel Macon deeply appreciated the political influence of a partisan press, and he was instrumental in establishing the *Raleigh Register* in 1799 under the skilled editorship of Joseph Gales. With his firm belief in Antifederalist principles, Macon remained a lifelong advocate of a free press as an essential defense against abuses by government and individuals.[19]

---

17. Elkins and McKitrick, *Age of Federalism*, 451-488; Banning, *Jeffersonian Persuasion*, 246; Saul Cornell, *The Other Founders: Antifederalism and the Dissenting Tradition in America, 1788-1828* (Chapel Hill: University of North Carolina Press, 1999), 177-178; Cunningham, *In Pursuit of Reason*, 171; Thomas P. Abernathy, *The South in the New Nation, 1789-1819* (Baton Rouge: Louisiana State University Press, 1961), 40, 128. As usual, Jefferson's own correspondence richly documents these matters. See Jefferson to James Madison, December 28, 1794, and Jefferson to Philip Mazzei, April 24, 1796, in Onuf, ed., *Jefferson: An Anthology*, 152-155.

18. Elkins and McKitrick, *Age of Federalism*, 282-288; Banning, *Jeffersonian Persuasion*, 167; Bailyn, *To Begin the World Anew*, 37-38. One scholar calls the 1790s a decade "when the political bloodletting seems to have been as harsh and shrill as at any time in our history." See Higginbotham, *Revolution in America*, 47.

19. Barry, "Nathaniel Macon," 67; Price, "Nathaniel Macon, Antifederalist," 300; Cornell, *The Other Founders*, 30-31, 106.

Secretary of the Treasury Alexander Hamilton argued for the creation of a national bank, the expansion of commerce and manufacturing, and a more conciliatory policy toward England. Jefferson worried that Washington increasingly supported Hamilton's positions. Frustrated with these developments, he resigned his cabinet position in 1793. Original portrait of Alexander Hamilton by Thomas Hamilton Crawford, 1860; published by Frost and Reed in 1932 (digital photograph from Prints and Photographs Division, Library of Congress, Washington, D.C.).

Shortly before Washington's retirement, one issue in particular had sharpened the division between Federalists and Republicans—the Jay Treaty. In the spring of 1794, Washington, in close consultation with Hamilton, had dispatched chief justice and Federalist leader John Jay to England to seek a treaty in which the British would abandon their remaining military posts in the Northwest, compensate American shippers for losses through naval seizures, pay American slave-holders for their property carried away in 1783, and allow unfettered commerce with the British West Indies. What Jay negotiated was less than satisfactory, even to some New England Federalists. England gained not only most-favored nation trading status but also the right to define neutrality in the ongoing dilemma of an America caught between the warring ships of Britain and France. Although England agreed to abandon its Northwest outposts by 1796 and to compensate recent American shipping losses, the concessions in the lucrative West Indian trade were so weak that the Senate ultimately rejected them. Finally, British claims for losses in the American Revolution could be claimed and paid by the American government, if so adjudicated, but planters' slave losses were not to be compensated.[20]

In the South, the Jay Treaty was the most despised feature of the Washington presidency, especially in North Carolina. Article IX of the treaty permitted British citizens to hold land in the U.S. Because North Carolina had earlier confiscated the immense holdings of Lord Granville in the northern half of the state, North Carolinians were deeply concerned about the future status of such real property. The treaty was just barely ratified by the two-thirds majority required in the Senate, and then the House was asked to appropriate funds to implement it.[21] Early in 1796 on the floor of the House, Nathaniel Macon spoke out against funding and said that thwarting the treaty was more important to his state than even the Declaration of Independence. After a hard fight, during which Macon earned the gratitude of Madison and other Republicans, the appropriation carried at the end of April. Only one member of the North Carolina delegation, ardent Federalist William Barry Grove of Fayetteville, voted for it. With Macon's growing prominence in Congress, North Carolina was moving steadily into the Republican ranks, with one brief interruption in 1798, when anti-French passions ran high.[22]

The radicalism of the French Revolutionaries, the British navy's growing insistence on preventing commerce between neutral nations and France, and the

---

20. Elkins and McKitrick, *Age of Federalism*, 396-414.

21. Abernathy, *The South in the New Nation*, 132-133, 225; Elkins and McKitrick, *Age of Federalism*, 415-426.

22. Delbert Harold Gilpatrick, *Jeffersonian Democracy in North Carolina, 1789-1816* (New York: Columbia University Press, 1931), 79-82; Dodd, *Life of Nathaniel Macon*, 86-87; Barry, "Nathaniel Macon," 41. Federalists won control of the state senate in 1798.

Virginia congressman James Madison shared Jefferson's alarm over the centralizing policies of Hamilton and Washington. Under a pen name, he frequently contributed strong editorial opinions to Philip Freneau's pro-Republican *National Gazette*. Original portrait of Madison by Gilbert Stuart; published by Pendleton's Lithography, ca. 1828 (digital photograph from Prints and Photographs Division, Library of Congress).

inexorable rise of Bonaparte were enormous problems for the still-young United States all through John Adams's presidency. Bitter partisan struggles at home exacerbated by international tensions split Republicans and Federalists even further. The Alien and Sedition Acts were symptomatic of these times.

By 1798, U.S. relations with France had degenerated into undeclared war on the open seas. America was plagued by the chaotic state of the French government, which was racked by internal and external enemies, as well as Gallic resentment over British gains through the Jay Treaty. President Adams tried to steer a careful course, but Hamiltonian allies in his own party demanded strong action. Congress increased the size of the army and ordered ships for the navy as appropriations—and the taxes to fund them—swelled. Republicans resented and resisted these measures, but they could not deny that the French government was far different than their ally of twenty years earlier or even just five years earlier, when something like a republic led by the beloved Lafayette might have prevailed.[23]

23. Elkins and McKitrick, *Age of Federalism*, 581-588. Macon consistently opposed the military and naval buildup in this period. Professional armies invited executive branch abuses and corrupt speculation by

In this heated atmosphere, the Federalist-dominated Congress enacted four measures in the summer of 1798 that Republicans felt were aimed directly at them and their supporters—the Alien and Sedition Acts. Three of the four bills comprising the acts manifested anger at resident foreigners, especially the French and Irish, who appeared to support Republicans. The legislation more than doubled the residence period required for citizenship and authorized the president to expel dangerous aliens. In truth, no one was ever deported under these measures, but their very passage—and Adams's acquiescence in them—infuriated Republicans. Macon opposed the bills heartily on the grounds that they perilously enhanced executive powers.[24]

A far greater threat than the Alien Acts was the Sedition Law. It forbade any conspiracy or combination directed at the federal government and prohibited writing, publishing, or speaking falsely or maliciously against the government. The highly partisan measure aimed at punishing the Republican press. Of the fourteen prosecutions that occurred under the law, all were aimed at Republicans. The only two Republican newspapers in New York City went out of business during this period, and every Republican publisher in the country felt threatened.[25]

In such an environment, Nathaniel Macon asserted himself more boldly than ever. He said in the initial debate on the Sedition Bill that it clearly violated the Constitution and added, "Laws of restraint, like this . . . always operate in a contrary direction from that which they were intended to take. The people suspect something is not right, when free discussion is feared by Government." Later in July, when the Senate's version of the bill came to the House, Macon continued to argue that it was unconstitutional. Review the ratification debate in the states, he advised. No prosecutions for libel by the national government were to occur: "Not a single member in any of the conventions gave an opinion to the contrary." Each state might choose to deal with libel through its own laws, but Congress could not.[26] Although the legislation passed, Republicans now had a rallying point that

civilian contractors. Navies were an undue tax burden that principally served mercantile, not agrarian, interests. He commended the role of Revolutionary War militias and privateers as the model for American defense against foreign enemies. See *Annals of Congress*, 5th Cong., 2nd sess., 1384-1386, 1465-1466, 1505-1507, 1671-1674, 1698-1699, 1756-1757.

24. Elkins and McKitrick, *Age of Federalism*, 591-592, 694-700; Barry, "Nathaniel Macon," 52. In North Carolina, anger at France had increased the power of Federalists in the state, and four of the ten congressmen elected in 1798 were Federalists. Still, William Barry Grove was the only member of the delegation to vote for the Alien and Sedition Acts. See James H. Broussard, "The North Carolina Federalists, 1800-1816," *North Carolina Historical Review* 55 (January 1978): 18-22; and Gilpatrick, *Jeffersonian Democracy in North Carolina*, 82, 91-92.

25. Elkins and McKitrick, *Age of Federalism*, 700-705; Banning, *Jeffersonian Persuasion*, 255-57; Joyce Appleby, *A Restless Past: History and the American Public* (Lanham, Md.: Rowman and Littlefield Publishers, 2005), 24; Cornell, *The Other Founders*, 231.

26. *Annals of Congress*, 5th Cong., 2nd sess., 2105-2106, 2151-2152. When Macon introduced a bill to repeal the Sedition Act early in 1800, he said, "The press is among the best gifts bestowed on man, its benefits are incalculable." See *Annals of Congress*, 6th Cong., 1st sess., 406.

By 1798, during the presidency of John Adams, U.S. relations with France had degenerated into undeclared war on the open seas. President Adams tried to steer a careful course, but the Federalist-dominated Congress enacted four measures in the summer of 1798 that Republicans felt were aimed directly at them and their supporters—the Alien and Sedition Acts. Adams's support for these bills infuriated Republicans, including Macon, who believed that they perilously enhanced executive powers. Portrait of Adams by Gilbert Stuart; engraving published by Pendleton's Lithography, ca. 1828 (digital photograph from American Memory, Library of Congress).

strengthened party loyalty. Albert Gallatin of Pennsylvania had succeeded Madison as Republican leader by 1797, and he and Macon became fast friends. Jefferson and Madison watched these developments closely and began to formulate their own rejoinders to what they saw as Federalist threats to a free government.[27] By the fall of 1798, Jefferson had written what would become a landmark in the formulation of a Republican creed—the Kentucky Resolutions.

The draft of the resolutions written in October asserted the rights of individual states to control their internal affairs and stressed that the federal government had specific powers defined by the Constitution—and no others. The initial resolution

---

27. Banning, *Jeffersonian Persuasion*, 249, 257; Barry, "Nathaniel Macon," 53-54, 57, 89; Malone, *Jefferson and the Ordeal of Liberty*, 395; Raymond Walters Jr., *Albert Gallatin: Jeffersonian Financier and Diplomat* (New York: Macmillan Co., 1957), 213.

declared that "the several States composing the United States are not united on the principle of unlimited submission to their General Government." Jefferson then proceeded to detail how the Alien and Sedition Acts were unconstitutional. In the eighth resolution, he argued: " where powers are assumed [by the General Government] which have not been delegated, a nullification of the act is the rightful remedy." The Alien and Sedition Acts, "unless arrested at the threshold, necessarily drive [the] States into revolution and blood."[28]

Jefferson had been wary of federal consolidation prior to ratification in 1787, and his subsequent experiences with Alexander Hamilton's loose interpretation of the Constitution had only underscored his concerns. Now in 1798, the Federalists' attack on individual freedoms led Jefferson to argue heatedly for severe limits on the national government. Indeed, when he sent his draft of the resolutions to James Madison, the younger man advised him to omit references to nullification and other overblown elements of the document. As finally adopted by the Kentucky legislature, the resolutions were milder than what Jefferson had originally proposed.[29]

Jefferson initially hoped that his resolutions would be adopted in North Carolina. In June 1798, John Taylor of Caroline had proposed that Virginia and its southern neighbor withdraw from the Union and form their own compact, but Jefferson rejected that idea on the grounds that future arguments between the two states would inevitably lead to further division. When North Carolinians, who deplored French interference in the Caribbean trade, turned their support to the Federalists, Jefferson accepted John Breckinridge's offer to introduce the resolutions in the Kentucky legislature.[30]

When no other state legislature adopted either the Kentucky Resolutions or Madison's more moderate Virginia Resolutions of December 1798, Jefferson staked out a doctrine of resistance to consolidation and affirmed the vital necessity of a local voice in governance. Early in 1799, he further refined these views in a letter to Elbridge Gerry of Massachusetts, espousing strict interpretation of the Constitution; opposition to "monarchical" tendencies that enhanced either the president or the Senate; promotion of frugality and simplicity in government; reduction of public debt; reliance on militias for defense "till actual invasions"; a small navy; "free commerce with all nations, political connections with none"; freedom of the press; and freedom of religion, including opposition to "a legal

---

28. Onuf, ed., *Jefferson: An Anthology*, 159-164.

29. Onuf, ed., *Jefferson: An Anthology*, 159-160; Malone, *Jefferson and the Ordeal of Liberty*, 402; Ellis, *American Sphinx*, 179. As was often the case, Jefferson's authorship of the resolutions was not widely known at the time.

30. Jefferson to John Taylor of Caroline, June 4, 1798, in Onuf, ed., *Jefferson: An Anthology*, 155-157; Abernathy, *The South in the New Nation*, 232-236; Malone, *Jefferson and the Ordeal of Liberty*, 401-402; Cornell, *The Other Founders*, 245.

ascendancy of one sect over another." When the Old Republicans began their break with Jefferson after 1805, they would hearken back to the "Spirit of '98" that the Gerry letter enunciated so clearly. Nathaniel Macon would endorse those principles, for they were already his own. For both men, the 1790s had been a decade when the ideals of individual liberty and political accountability so central to the American Revolution had been eroded and threatened. Jefferson, and to a lesser extent Macon, were less states' rights advocates in the way that southerners of the 1850s would be than men who supported state sovereignty at a time when the federal government seemed to be leaning toward monarchy.[31]

With Jefferson's election as president in 1800 and Republican control of Congress, the "Revolution of 1800," as Jefferson would call it years later, was under way. In the House of Representatives, Nathaniel Macon was elected Speaker late in 1801, and he eventually elevated John Randolph of Roanoke to chairmanship of the powerful Ways and Means Committee. The Seventh Congress, with Macon in the Speaker's chair, approved a bill to completely retire the public debt by 1817, reduced the army to three thousand troops, and cut naval appropriations. As Macon's ally Joseph Nicholson of Maryland said in the first session, "It is no part of our political creed that a public debt is a public blessing."[32] The "Spirit of '98" was being put into practice.

Months earlier, just after Jefferson was installed as president (which was carried out with little fanfare in marked contrast to the inauguration of John Adams), Nathaniel Macon had written to his friend: "Suffer me to say to you that the people expect—That Levees will be done way / That the communication to the next Congress will be by letter not a speech / That we have too many ministers in Europe / . . . That the army might be safely reduced. . . . In fact that a system of economy is to be adopted and pursued with energy."[33]

Jefferson's response on May 14, 1801, delighted Macon: "Levees are done away. The first communication to the next Congress will be, like all subsequent ones, by message, to which no answer will be expected. The diplomatic establishment in Europe will be reduced to three ministers." Both Macon's April letter and the president's reply grew directly out of their creed: wariness of the executive and any tendencies toward monarchical practices, as well as frugality—leading to lower taxes—in the operations of government. Both Jefferson and Macon disliked the

---

31. Jefferson to Elbridge Gerry, January 26, 1799, in Onuf, ed., *Jefferson: An Anthology*, 164-169; Cunningham, *In Pursuit of Reason*, 166; Malone, *Jefferson and the Ordeal of Liberty*, 409; Ellis, *American Sphinx*, 254.

32. Wilentz, *The Rise of American Democracy*, 98; Barry, "Nathaniel Macon," 78-79; Banning, *Jeffersonian Persuasion*, 277.

33. Macon to Jefferson, April 20, 1801, Jefferson Papers; Wilentz, *The Rise of American Democracy*, 95. On Inauguration Day, Jefferson, in a plain suit and with his hair unpowdered, walked from his lodgings to the Capitol and was sworn in.

formal receptions (called levees) conducted by Washington and then Adams, which they scorned as a despicable aspect of Crown rule. Macon also felt that presidents should respect the separate branch status of Congress by avoiding personal appearances there. Because Jefferson's public speaking abilities were notoriously weak, and he heartily rejected royalist pretensions, he undoubtedly welcomed Macon's suggestion to communicate with the legislative branch in writing.[34]

It was in this atmosphere that Jefferson's supporters, who detested the pro-British sympathies among many Federalists, believed their Revolution of 1800 had reasserted the values of the American Revolution. John Randolph of Roanoke spoke for Macon and others when he recalled Jefferson's first term, especially its first two years, "as the true republican interlude in American government."[35] During Jefferson's first four years as president, he and Macon were more closely bound than they ever would be by creed and politics. They shared a disdain for undue enhancement of the executive, distrust of a professional army and navy, dread of debt and financial speculation, faith in the good sense of most Americans living and working on their own farms, and respect for the rights and necessity of state sovereignty. Jefferson confronted the problems and opportunities of presidential leadership with his keen intellect and ambition, and he inevitably altered some of his views in his second term, but Macon continued to maintain and assert those early principles throughout his life, reflecting not only his legislative-branch perspective but also his deepest political convictions.

As Jefferson faced the complex tasks of governing a nation, he reevaluated many of his earlier criticisms of the presidency. His policies on foreign relations, Indians, territorial expansion, and promoting commerce and manufacturing—despite his agrarian ideals—often troubled his political allies. He seemed disposed to let the issues of 1798 fade away as the actualities of his office and the bitter opposition of Federalists sank in.[36] During 1805, Jefferson's cousin and Macon intimate John Randolph of Roanoke was ready to break with the president. Randolph had been troubled by the scheming and fraud that surrounded the Yazoo land speculations in Georgia. Jefferson tried to settle the dispute because investors were from various states, not just one. But the definitive split between the two men came in December, when the president sought two million dollars from

---

34. Jefferson to Macon, May 14, 1801, Jefferson Papers; Barry, "Nathaniel Macon," 75; Cunningham, *In Pursuit of Reason*, 247, 257. Cunningham writes that Jefferson abandoned the practice of delivering the annual message to Congress in person less because of his poor speaking voice than because of Macon's letter. Presidents maintained this practice until 1913.

35. Dawidoff, *Education of John Randolph*, 156, 172; Malone, *Jefferson and the Ordeal of Liberty*, 265-266; Wilentz, *The Rise of American Democracy*, 172.

36. Risjord, *Old Republicans*, 24; Wilentz, *The Rise of American Democracy*, 104-108; Banning, *Jeffersonian Persuasion*, 284-285.

Congress to obtain West Florida from Spain by involving agents of Napoleon's government. From then on, Randolph became a near-inflexible opponent of any of Jefferson's initiatives. Allied with Randolph was a group of a half dozen or so adherents of the "Spirit of '98," including Nathaniel Macon, soon dubbed Quids or Old Republicans.[37]

Although Macon was Randolph's lifelong friend—and lost a fourth term as Speaker largely because he refused to abandon his quick-tempered comrade—he never hesitated to differ with Randolph when he felt the need. Indeed, it is not a simple matter to define Macon as a Quid. Conservative, yes; wary of presidential power, yes; a devotee of the "Spirit of '98," to be sure; yet Macon never thoroughly broke with Jefferson as Randolph did. Macon did not hesitate to vote with the president when he agreed with his proposals.[38] There is a telling letter from the president to the Speaker during a time when the Old Republicans were asserting themselves early in 1806: "Some enemy, whom we know not, is sowing tares among us. Between you & myself nothing but opportunities of explanation can be necessary to defeat those endeavors. At least on my part, my confidence in you is so unqualified that nothing further is necessary for my satisfaction. I must therefore ask a conversation with you. This evening my company may stay late: but tomorrow evening, or the next I can be alone." Whether or not Macon accepted the invitation is unknown, but Jefferson's sentiments demonstrate a level of affection and respect that honored Macon and that he, without fanfare, reciprocated.[39]

Jefferson's second term in the White House was complicated by growing tensions with England, locked as it was in the Napoleonic Wars. In the summer of 1807, a British warship fired on the American *Chesapeake* off the Virginia capes, killing three and wounding eighteen. The nation was incensed, and the president shared in the anger and wanted a forceful response. However, Jefferson was fully aware that the United States could not challenge Britain on the high seas. With the encouragement of Secretary of State James Madison, the president late in 1807 proposed an embargo that would prohibit all maritime trade with foreign nations.

37. Abernathy, *The South in the New Nation*, 313-314; Wilentz, *The Rise of American Democracy*, 108, 124; Dawidoff, *Education of John Randolph*, 200.

38. Richard E. Ellis, *The Jeffersonian Crisis: Courts and Politics in the Young Republic* (New York: Oxford University Press, 1971), 237; Risjord, *Old Republicans*, 65-66. On Macon's friendship with Randolph, see Price, "Nathaniel Macon, Planter," 199-201, 204. The two men frequently lodged together in the same boardinghouse in Washington when Congress was in session and spent many pleasant evenings enjoying the hospitality of Albert Gallatin in his gracious home on Capitol Hill. See Walters, *Albert Gallatin*, 148; and Barry, "Nathaniel Macon," 89, 95.

39. Jefferson to Macon, March 26, 1806, in Ford, ed., *Writings of Thomas Jefferson*, 8:439; Dumas Malone, *Jefferson the President: Second Term, 1805-1809* (Boston: Little, Brown and Co., 1974), 112. Jefferson often used informal dinners at the White House to discuss matters with allies and others. He used a dumbwaiter to serve dishes himself so that not even servants would disturb—or overhear—private conversations. See Young, *The Washington Community*, 168-170.

Jefferson reasoned that, if nothing else, the embargo would buy time for America to prepare for war. Congress quickly enacted the measure, but it began to unravel almost immediately. Mercantile interests, especially in the Northeast, regularly circumvented the prohibitions. Early in 1809, as Jefferson's presidency drew to a close, a congressional alliance of New Englanders, New Yorkers, and Southern Quids put an end to the embargo. When Jefferson left the White House in March 1809, he was relieved to be retiring from the political fray. As he wrote to a friend shortly before relinquishing office, "Within a few days I retire to my family, my books, and farms; and having gained the harbor myself, I shall look to my friends still buffeting the storm, with anxiety indeed, but not with envy. Never did a prisoner, released from his chains, feel such relief as I shall on shaking off the shackles of power." As a recent biographer of Jefferson notes, "[His] second term had proved as disastrous as his first term had been glorious." He would never return to Washington.[40]

Unlike Randolph, who initially supported the embargo then vehemently resisted it, Macon endorsed the measure. He missed voting for it in 1807 because of illness, but he always favored the embargo as the most pragmatic approach to rebutting England. British depredations at sea inflamed Macon, who considered the attack on the *Chesapeake* to be an act of war. Still, he opposed raising a navy as impractical as well as too expensive. The nation would do better to contract with privateers than to assume the costs of ship and port construction, salaried officers and men, supply depots, and more. Although he supported Jefferson on the embargo, Macon opposed his plan to outfit a series of defensive (and relatively inexpensive) gunboats to protect coastal waters. What he objected to was not the boats themselves, but rather that the legislation authorized the president to man the vessels without first seeking congressional approval.[41]

Shortly after Jefferson's retirement, Macon said, "I feel no hesitation in saying that the nation will never be blessed with another such administration as the last." Despite this warm assessment, Macon refused to budge from his lifelong opposition to special favors. He was the sole member of Congress to oppose granting Jefferson postal franking privileges when he left office, and he was one of only fifteen Republicans to vote against purchasing the contents of the great man's personal library to replace losses after the British set fire to Washington during the War of 1812. No doubt Jefferson viewed Macon's votes as perfectly consistent with the

40. Wilentz, *The Rise of American Democracy*, 130-135; Jefferson to P. S. Dupont de Nemours March 2, 1809, in Onuf, ed., *Jefferson: An Anthology*, 212 (first quotation); Ellis, *American Sphinx*, 238 (second quotation).

41. Barry, "Nathaniel Macon," 124-128; *Annals of Congress*, 10th Cong., 1st sess., 1028-1029; Macon to Albert Gallatin, July 12, 1807, Albert Gallatin Papers, New-York Historical Society, New York City (photocopies in State Archives, North Carolina Office of Archives and History, Raleigh).

North Carolinian's confirmed stances against anything that smacked of favoritism. In a republic, no citizen stood above others.[42]

Back home in Monticello, Jefferson settled into the relative quiet of the mountaintop estate, in marked contrast to his life in Washington. Yet he was far from being isolated. Surrounded by family and a large slave population, Jefferson had plenty of human contact. Moreover, there was a steady flow of guests and tourists ranging from foreign dignitaries to curious travelers hoping for a glimpse of the great man. Some nights as many as fifty people gathered under his roof. In addition to this traffic during the warm-weather months, Jefferson also maintained a massive correspondence. He received more than a thousand letters each year (in 1820, he counted 1,267 of them) and spent three or four hours daily responding to them. In his last decade, he devoted most of his time to establishing the University of Virginia in nearby Charlottesville. From rallying political support to designing buildings, to defining curriculum, to hiring faculty, Jefferson was involved in every major—and many minor—aspects of an enterprise that he came to see as a crowning achievement.[43]

Jefferson became increasingly alarmed about the nation's welfare after the War of 1812. With the peace in 1815, divisions between an expanding commercial North and a predominantly agrarian South became more starkly evident with each passing year. With westward expansion, new territories began applying for admission as states, and the country confronted issues about the legal status of slavery. When Missouri sought statehood in 1819, a congressman from New York proposed that slavery ultimately be prohibited there. Over the next year, the debates that swirled around this question exposed a deep rift in the country that would culminate with the Civil War. Both Jefferson and Macon feared that as the federal government further consolidated power, states—especially slave states— would gradually lose the power to manage their internal affairs. They firmly believed that emancipation would lead to chaos and anarchy.[44]

---

42. Dumas Malone, *The Sage of Monticello* (Boston: Little, Brown and Co., 1981), 24, 178; J. Jefferson Looney, ed., *The Papers of Thomas Jefferson: Retirement Series*, 3 vols. to date (Princeton, N.J.: Princeton University Press, 2004-), 1:191n, 349; Price, "Nathaniel Macon, Planter," 211.

43. Ellis, *American Sphinx*, 232, 280-287; Onuf, ed., *Jefferson: An Anthology*, 240-244.

44. Wilentz, *The Rise of American Democracy*, 221-230; Ellis, *American Sphinx*, 264-268; Barry, "Nathaniel Macon," 219-222. Like many American Revolutionaries, Jefferson and Macon deplored the existence of slavery but embraced it through their ownership of slaves (whom they believed to be racially inferior) and as a given of plantation economy and culture. There are many studies of Jefferson and slavery. The best starting point is Winthrop D. Jordan, *White over Black: American Attitudes toward the Negro, 1550-1812* (Chapel Hill: University of North Carolina Press, 1968), 429-481. For an informative, concise view, see Elizabeth Fox-Genovese and Eugene D. Genovese, *The Mind of the Master Class: History and Faith in the Southern Slaveholders' Worldview* (New York: Cambridge University Press, 2005), 78-80. See pages 5 and 69 for the Genoveses' instructive perspective on viewing slaveholders in the context of their own times. On Macon's views, see Price, "Nathaniel Macon, Planter," 201-204.

During the debates in 1820, Senator Macon argued that the federal government had no right to prohibit slavery in Missouri and that the voters there should ultimately decide the institution's fate. "Why leave the road of experience which has satisfied all, and made all happy, to take this new way of which we have no experience? The way leads to universal emancipation of which we have no experience," Macon said. He also rejected the idea that Jefferson's "all men are created equal" phrase of 1776 applied to the Missouri debates, asking, "follow that sentiment, and does it not lead to universal emancipation? If it will justify putting an end to slavery in Missouri, will it not justify it in the old States?"[45]

Back at Monticello, Jefferson had followed the debates with growing alarm and agitation. More than one visitor commented on how disturbed the old man was by the whole enterprise. After a year of turmoil, a congressional compromise in March 1820 admitted Maine and Missouri into the Union as free and slave states, respectively, and prohibited slavery in future northern territories. In April, Jefferson wrote to John Holmes of Maine, "this momentous question, like a fire bell in the night, awakened and filled me with terror. I considered it as the knell of the Union. It is hushed, indeed for the moment. But this is a reprieve only, not a final sentence." After briefly expressing a hope that in the future some general emancipation might be effected, Jefferson articulated the dilemma facing every defender of slavery: "we have the wolf by the ears, and we can neither hold him, nor safely let him go. Justice is in the one scale, and self-preservation in the other."[46]

After the Missouri Compromise, Jefferson lived six more years, and Macon served eight more years in the Senate. Each man continued in his role as a planter, an admired political sage, and a valued correspondent in what they both called their "old age." They never abandoned their commitment to the Union formed in the American Revolution, but both clearly feared for the future of their region and for their vision of the liberty won from England in 1783. For Jefferson as well as Macon, a deep aversion to remote authority and its power lay at the core of the Revolutionary legacy. They watched uneasily as the nation they helped to launch began to expand economically and geographically after 1815. Both feared that increased federal power and burgeoning national expenditures would lead to the corruption they had so despised in royal government.[47]

45. *Annals of Congress*, 16th Cong., 1st sess., 225-226; Wilentz, *The Rise of American Democracy*, 230-232; Price, "Nathaniel Macon, Antifederalist," 309.

46. John Chester Miller, *The Wolf by the Ears: Thomas Jefferson and Slavery* (New York: The Free Press, 1977), 228-233; Jefferson to John Holmes, April 22, 1820, in Onuf, ed., *Jefferson: An Anthology*, 244-245. As early as 1818, Macon had told Bartlett Yancey that emancipation "will destroy our beloved mother N. Carolina and all the South country." Quoted in Barry, "Nathaniel Macon," 209.

47. Ellis, *American Sphinx*, 295-296; Bailyn, *To Begin the World Anew*, 55; Watson, *Liberty and Power*, 8.

This copy of Macon's bookplate is from an eighteenth-century volume of satirical verse in the author's collection and matches that of some books held by the North Carolina Museum of History. The bookplate features the Latinized spelling of "Nathanael," as opposed to the Hebrew-inspired "Nathaniel." Macon, whom Jefferson called "the last of the Romans" and whom Thomas Hart Benton called "the real Cincinnatus of America," possibly chose this bookplate to reflect his admiration of the Roman past.

For example, Jefferson wrote to an associate late in 1825, "I see, as you do, with the greatest affliction, the rapid strides with which the federal government is advancing towards the usurpation of all the rights reserved to the States." He then went on to berate the executive and judicial branches for their loose interpretation of the Constitution and the Congress for not standing up to them. Yet he equally opposed any hot-tempered talk of dissolution: "That must be the last resource." For now, the states had to patiently hope that the sheer accumulation of federal wrongs would bring the nation's electorate to its senses. Less than three years later, Macon echoed some of these sentiments in notes written for remarks he delivered in his last year in the Senate: "Every extension of power by construction makes the operation of government more unequal, the [Constitutional] convention aware of this gave but few powers, that convention knew [the] difficulty of managing an unlimited federative Govt.—a majority may be tyrants." He also said, " I have loved [the] Union [and] wish to die loving it."[48] Old Revolutionaries like Jefferson and Macon could sense the prospect of a future civil war, and they dreaded it. They were still "union men" and hoped that a reconciliation between the nation and the states might yet be effected. Jefferson and Macon never wavered in upholding a cardinal principle of the Revolution—that the people were sovereign and that their good sense would finally prevail.[49]

48. Jefferson to William Branch Giles, December 26, 1825, in Onuf, ed., *Jefferson: An Anthology*, 253-254; undated [but likely 1828] notes in Macon's hand in Katherine Clark Pendleton Conway Collection, Private Collections, State Archives.

49. Wood, *Creation of the American Republic*, 614; Ellis, *American Sphinx*, 9-10. Macon's stance is more fully treated in Price, "Nathaniel Macon, Antifederalist," 307-310. Also see Macon's comments at the 1835 Constitutional Convention in *Proceedings and Debates of the Convention of North-Carolina Called to Amend the Constitution of the State, which Assembled at Raleigh, June 4, 1835* (Raleigh, N.C.: Joseph Gales and Son, 1836), 176-177.

Jefferson and Macon maintained an intermittent, cordial correspondence after 1815. Whatever wounds there were from Jefferson's second term and Macon's loss of the speakership had healed. Interestingly, their letters resumed because of art, not politics. On January 7, 1816, Macon wrote to Monticello asking Jefferson to recommend a sculptor for a full-size statue of George Washington to be placed in the Capitol in Raleigh. The artist should preferably be an American of top quality, but if no such person existed, then a European, surely Italian. Macon concluded warmly, "That the evening of your life may be as happy as the meridian has been useful, is [my] sincere prayer." A seven-year silence between the two now broken, Jefferson responded with a long letter on January 22 recommending the Italian Antonio Canova as the best sculptor currently working. He noted that there was presently no American sculptor of the first rank and that Italian marble was top quality. Jefferson, who a decade later would deem Macon the "Last of the Romans," further suggested that Washington be garbed as an ancient Roman rather than in his American uniform, observing, "our boots and regimentals have a very puny effect."[50]

After 1819, exchanges between the two men largely concentrated on political concerns. Addressing Macon "as the Depository of old & sound principles," Jefferson wrote to the senator in the summer of 1821 suggesting that Congress protest the federal judiciary's invasion of states' rights and proceed to impeachments should the objections go unheeded. He further urged that Congress cease borrowing to pay the national debt: "If this cannot be done without dismissing the army & putting ships out of commission, haul them up high & dry, and reduce the army to the lowest point at which it was ever established." Macon responded in kind two months later: "for two years past, the U-S have borrowed money in time of peace to keep their vessels cruising on every sea, & to pay an army; but G. Britain does the same; and if we continue to follow her example, debt, taxes & grinding the poor are certain consequences." The sentiments of both men were profoundly linked to their Revolutionary legacy of hatred of a military establishment, burdensome taxes, and public debt leading inevitably to financial speculation, corruption, and loss of civic virtue.[51]

In his retirement and much alarmed by the widening national rift exposed in the Missouri Compromise, Jefferson moved closer to Macon's conservatism than at any time since 1798. As the Sage of Monticello wrote to the senator late in 1823

50. Macon to Jefferson, January 7, 1816, and Jefferson to Macon, January 22, 1816, Jefferson Papers. When the Capitol burned in 1831, the Canova Washington was damaged beyond repair. A replacement made from the original model in Italy was installed in the present Capitol in 1970 with Washington in Roman military dress. See William S. Powell, *North Carolina through Four Centuries* (Chapel Hill: University of North Carolina Press, 1989), 213-214.

51. Jefferson to Macon, August 19, 1821, in Ford, ed., *Writings of Thomas Jefferson*, 10:192-193 Macon to Jefferson, October 20, 1821, Jefferson Papers; McDonald, *Novus Ordo Seclorum*, 74-77.

In 1816, Macon asked Jefferson to recommend a sculptor for a full-size statue of George Washington to be placed in the Capitol in Raleigh. The Italian sculptor Antonio Canova, Jefferson wrote back, was the best currently working, and Italian marble was of the highest quality. Jefferson suggested that Washington be garbed as an ancient Roman rather than in his American uniform. Canova's original sculpture of George Washington stood in the rotunda of the State Capitol from 1820 to 1831 when it was severely damaged in a fire in 1831. This copy replaced the original in 1970. Photograph by Alan Westmoreland for the State Archives, North Carolina Office of Archives and History, Raleigh.

For his grave, Jefferson requested that an unadorned obelisk be inscribed with three achievements for which he wished to be remembered: his authorship of the Declaration of Independence and of the Virginia Statute for Religious Freedom, and his fatherhood of the University of Virginia. The original obelisk marker for Jefferson's grave was moved from Monticello to the University of Missouri at Columbia in the 1880s, replaced by this marker. Photograph by Christopher Hollis for Wdwic Pictures, July 2001; reproduced by permission.

in introducing his physician to Macon, "his political principles are yours and mine . . . he naturally wishes to be known to one so long and so prominent in the school of genuine republicanism."[52] Three years later, in the letter already noted in which Jefferson introduced his grandson to Macon, he called the senator a model of "genuine republicanism." What did Jefferson mean by the term?

Like other veterans of the heady times of the American Revolution, neither Jefferson nor Macon precisely defined republicanism. For them, it was less a formal structure than a spirit of government, and the ideal government was republican.

52. Jefferson to Macon, October 10, 1823, Jefferson Papers.

ESSE QUAM VIDERI

NATHANIEL MACON
1758 - 1837
A SOLDIER OF THE REVOLUTION; STATE SENATOR.
1782 AND 1784; REPRESENTATIVE IN CONGRESS.
1791-1815. AND SPEAKER OF THE HOUSE.1801-1807;
UNITED STATES SENATOR. 1815-1828. AND PRESIDENT
PRO TEM OF THE SENATE. 1826-1828. PRESIDENT OF THE
CONSTITUTIONAL CONVENTION OF 1835."THE STRICTEST
OF OUR MODELS OF GENUINE REPUBLICANISM.
NATHANIEL MACON, UPON WHOSE TOMB WILL BE
WRITTEN. 'ULTIMUS ROMANORUM.'"-THOMAS JEFFERSON.

ERECTED 1919 BY THE
NORTH CAROLINA HISTORICAL COMMISSION
AND
MACON NORTH CAROLINA COMMUNITY CLUB

Macon requested that his grave be unmarked, except for stones tossed on it out of the plow's path, but in 1919, the North Carolina Historical Commission disregarded Macon's instructions and erected a large bronze plaque on granite as a headstone. Photograph from the State Archives.

Like Plutarch's ancient Greeks and Romans whom they so admired, the virtues of restraint, courage, dignity, and personal independence characterized the leaders of a republic. Hereditary nobility and aristocracy weakened society through their extravagance and pursuit of personal gain. The rustic, self-sufficient yeoman was the ideal. In a monarchy, a man's desire to be virtuous was often discouraged; in a republic, each citizen subsumed "his personal wants into the good of the whole."[53]

After leaving the White House, Jefferson came to believe increasingly that republicanism relied on direct and vigilant control by the citizenry. Voluntary consent by the governed was key, and the best government was that one closest to the electorate. He saw the federal courts as furthest removed from the people, followed by the Senate, the president, the House of Representatives, the state legislatures, and finally the local governments, where voters could meet face-to-face

53. Wood, *Creation of the American Republic*, 48-53, 68. Helpful to understanding the persistence of these issues (as well as nationalist vs. states' rights struggles) is the concise treatment in Akhil Reed Amar, *The Bill of Rights: Creation and Reconstruction* (New Haven, Conn.: Yale University Press, 1998), 4-11.

with those governing. Whatever acted to make government more remote from the people was undesirable. Although Jefferson never quite equaled the Antifederalist stance of Macon, he got closer to it each year from 1816 until his death. As he wrote to Macon in the winter of 1826, "I am particularly happy to perceive that you retain health and spirits manfully to maintain our good old principles of cherishing and fortifying the rights and authorities of the people in opposition to those who fear them, who wish to take all power from them, and to transfer all to Washington."[54]

When death took Jefferson on July 4, 1826, the fiftieth anniversary of American independence, his family soon discovered in his personal effects his designs for a gravestone. An unadorned obelisk was to be inscribed with those achievements for which Jefferson wished to be remembered: his authorship of the Declaration of Independence and of the Virginia Statute for Religious Freedom, and his fatherhood of the University of Virginia. He did not mention his terms as president of the United States nor of any other office, elected or appointed.[55]

Nathaniel Macon died eleven years later. Befitting his more Spartan tastes, he insisted that his grave be unmarked, save for stones tossed on it out of the plow's path. In 1919, the North Carolina Historical Commission disregarded Macon's instructions and erected a large bronze plaque on granite as a headstone. Of its nine lines of text describing Macon's achievements, four are drawn from Jefferson's final letter to him: "The Strictest of Our Models of Genuine Republicanism, Nathaniel Macon, Upon Whose Tomb Will Be Written, 'Ultimus Romanorum.' "[56] Yes, Macon's last wishes were broken, but there is a measure of solace in knowing that the words of an old and valued friend stand near his bones.

54. Ellis, *American Sphinx*, 259-262; Barry, "Nathaniel Macon," 191-193; Price, "Nathaniel Macon, Antifederalist," 300-301; Jefferson to Macon, February 21, 1826, in Ford, ed., *Writings of Thomas Jefferson*, 10:378-379.

55. Malone, *The Sage of Monticello*, 498-499.

56. Price, "Nathaniel Macon, Planter," 213-214, describes Macon's instructions and has a picture of the grave.

Nathaniel Macon, Antifederalist

—◆◆◆—

On March 25, 1839, the president of the United States wrote to a group of supporters who had invited him to a public dinner in his honor in Warrenton, North Carolina. Martin Van Buren said that the press of the nation's business would curtail his spring travel plans but that their generous invitation was welcome because it came "from the immediate friends and neighbors of the late Nathaniel Macon; from those who have been familiar with the counsels, and nurtured in the principles of that great and good man, whose friendship it was my happiness to enjoy for many years, and until the day of his death." Fifteen years later in the turbulent decade of the 1850s, Van Buren would note in his auto-biography that there was no one whose opinion he valued more than "the venerable Macon."[1]

For his part, Nathaniel Macon had worked closely with Van Buren in Democratic politics in the 1820s and beyond and had liked the "Little Magician." Macon's last official act was to vote for Van Buren's presidency as an elector in 1836, and his last letter was one sent to the new chief executive the next year.[2] Van Buren recognized Macon's stature among the Old Republicans (the conservative wing of the party of Thomas Jefferson) as well as throughout the South, and during the late 1820s he purposely courted Dixie. When the Little Magician traveled southward in 1827 garnering support for the presidential campaign of Andrew Jackson, he sought Macon's advice. Macon had long been suspicious of Old Hickory as more ambitious than principled, but he trusted Van Buren's commitment to strict constructionism and states' rights. Ultimately, Macon would come to admire much of Jackson's

1. Martin Van Buren to Henry Fitts and others, March 25, 1839, Martin Van Buren Papers, Library of Congress, Washington, D.C. (typed transcripts in Private Collections, State Archives, North Carolina Office of Archives and History, Raleigh), hereinafter cited as Van Buren Papers; John C. Fitzpatrick, ed., *Autobiography of Martin Van Buren* (Washington, D.C.: Government Printing Office, 1920), 221.

2. William S. Price Jr., "Nathaniel Macon, Planter," *North Carolina Historical Review* 78 (April 2001): 201-204, 207, 210; Stephen J. Barry, "Nathaniel Macon: The Prophet of Pure Republicanism, 1758-1837" (Ph.D. diss., State University of New York at Buffalo, 1995), 293; William S. Hoffmann, *Andrew Jackson and North Carolina Politics* (Chapel Hill: University of North Carolina Press, 1958), 104.

presidency, and Van Buren's prominent role in the administration surely swayed Macon's favor.[3]

What was it that bound the slaveholding "most typical" North Carolinian of his era (as W. E. Dodd called Macon) to a New Yorker of Dutch ancestry who would in 1848 become the presidential candidate of the Free-Soilers? As different as both men were—culturally, geographically, socially—they shared a common political ideology born of Antifederalism.[4]

As its name proclaims, Antifederalism sprang from the controversy surrounding ratification of the federal Constitution of 1787.[5] Opponents of that document feared in its greater centralization of national authority many of the same things that had led them to revolt in 1775. For them the more expansive the authority of any government, the more removed it was from the governed and the more certainly it would tend toward corruption and tyranny. Power was dominion and ultimately compulsion; its natural prey was liberty. Power was aggressive; liberty, passive. Thus, liberty had to be defended. The purpose of good government was to assure the attainment of liberty, but only the vigilance of the governed protected liberty because government, through its officers, would inevitably seek to subvert it. As the colonists had rallied against George III in 1775 because his "corrupt ministers" had upset the balanced English constitution of kings, lords, and commons, so Antifederalists in 1787 would oppose what they saw as a strengthened national executive, a weakened Congress, and an undermining of individual state sovereignty. The earlier specter of standing armies, an established church, unreasonable taxes, executive patronage, and a remote central authority that had been so feared by Revolutionaries in 1775 resurfaced among Antifederalists in 1787.[6]

3. Donald B. Cole, *Martin Van Buren and the American Political System* (Princeton, N.J.: Princeton University Press, 1984), 110; John Niven, *Martin Van Buren: The Romantic Age of American Politics* (New York: Oxford University Press, 1983), 179-183; Norman K. Risjord, *The Old Republicans: Southern Conservatism in the Age of Jefferson* (New York: Columbia University Press, 1965), 262, 280-281; Barry, "Nathaniel Macon," 265-269.

4. William E. Dodd, *The Life of Nathaniel Macon* (Raleigh, N.C.: Edwards and Broughton, 1903), 399; Barry, "Nathaniel Macon," vi, 30; Saul Cornell, *The Other Founders: Anti-Federalism and the Dissenting Tradition in America, 1788-1828* (Chapel Hill: Published for the Omohundro Institute of Early American History and Culture by the University of North Carolina Press, 1999), 298-299, 302.

5. The historical literature on the Antifederalists is deep and wide. Many of the best sources are ably treated in Gaspare J. Saladino, "The Bill of Rights: A Bibliographical Essay," in *The Bill of Rights and the States: The Colonial and Revolutionary Origins of American Liberties*, ed. Patrick T. Conley and John P. Kaminski (Madison, Wis.: Madison House, 1992), 478-482. The most helpful study of Antifederalism published since Saladino's overview is Saul Cornell's *Other Founders*, cited above. Especially instructive is Cornell's treatment of the persistence of Antifederalism well beyond ratification in 1789.

6. Bernard Bailyn, ed., *Pamphlets of the American Revolution, 1750-1776*, volume 1: *1750-1765* (Cambridge, Mass.: Belknap Press of Harvard University Press, 1965), 38-40, 46; Forrest McDonald, *Novus Ordo Seclorum: The Intellectual Origins of the Constitution* (Lawrence: University Press of Kansas, 1985), 25-26, 76-78; Stanley Elkins and Eric McKitrick, *The Age of Federalism* (New York: Oxford

Warren County native Nathaniel Macon served in the U.S. Congress for thirty-seven years—twenty-four in the House and thirteen in the Senate. A veteran of the Revolution, Macon was an ardent Antifederalist throughout his life. Robert D. Gauley portrait of Nathaniel Macon courtesy of the Architect of the Capitol, Washington, D.C. The painting is located in the Speakers Lobby and is part of the U.S. House of Representatives collection.

A major dread of Antifederalists was consolidation. Proposals to share power between the nation and the states would inevitably lead to a federal government dictating to the smaller units. Political centralization fostered economic centralization, which in turn spurred moral decay in the unbridled pursuit of wealth. The Constitution of 1787 threatened to generate an aristocracy in the executive and the Senate, judicial tyranny in federal courts that would override state courts, oppression through taxation powers, and more. Of enormous concern was the absence of a bill of rights guaranteeing individual freedoms. Finally, there was the crucial matter of the *size* of government; the Antifederalist ideal was a small republic. There, virtuous men who understood the public interest and were known to their constituents would rise to positions of authority. This happy situation could occur only if politics were rooted in localities. A national government was

University Press, 1993), 6-7, 10-12; John P. Kaminski, "The Constitution without a Bill of Rights," in Conley and Kaminski, eds., *The Bill of Rights and the States*, 16-26.

too disparate and diverse to be able to detect the popular will. State governments were closer physically and culturally to the governed.[7]

One point on which Federalists and Antifederalists could agree was who should have a voice in government—adult males with a stake in society manifested through property ownership or payment of taxes.[8] While government would represent this constituency of propertied males and their subordinates, the nature of that government would be the scene of battle between Federalists and Antifederalists through various permutations, including the formation of political parties, for decades to come, right down to today.

If Federalists viewed ratification in 1789 as their victory, Antifederalists applauded the approval of the Bill of Rights in 1791. After that, Antifederalists would lose their initial reason for being but would continue to exist in a persistent network of resistance that ultimately led to the creation of the Democratic-Republicans as a party opposing the Federalists.[9]

By the fall of 1791, a discernible opposition to certain programs of President George Washington's administration began to emerge as the competing political visions of Alexander Hamilton and Thomas Jefferson vied. This was the same year in which Nathaniel Macon first appeared in Congress. Rival newspapers like the pro-Hamilton *Gazette of the United States* and the pro-Jefferson *National Gazette* hurled stinging editorials and stories at one another throughout 1792. The elections of that fall were contested on a near-partisan basis. In ensuing years, struggles like those over the Jay Treaty with Britain, the Quasi War with France, and the Alien and Sedition Acts had generated clearly defined factions by 1798. Nathaniel Macon would align himself with the Republicans (as they were then called), led by Thomas Jefferson and James Madison, authors of the Kentucky and Virginia Resolutions, respectively. Both texts, written at the close of 1798, argued for strict construction of the Constitution and individual state sovereignty. Their philosophies borrowed much from the rhetoric of Antifederalism a decade earlier.[10]

Nathaniel Macon was born, bred, resided, and died in a colony, later a state, whose spirited opposition to federalism in the ratification debates of 1787-1789 epitomized its ongoing resistance to distant ruling authority. Of the thirteen

---

7. Eugene D. Genovese, *The Southern Tradition: The Achievement and Limitations of an American Conservatism* (Cambridge, Mass.: Harvard University Press, 1994), 85, 95, 97; Cornell, *Other Founders*, 11, 30-31, 58, 62-63, 80.

8. McDonald, *Novus Ordo Seclorum*, 74-75; Russell Kirk, *Randolph of Roanoke: A Study in Conservative Thought* (Chicago: University of Chicago Press, 1951), 26.

9. Elkins and McKitrick, *Age of Federalism*, 257-270.

10. Elkins and McKitrick, *Age of Federalism*, 257, 282, 288, 441-442, 591-592, 719-720, 726; Genovese, *The Southern Tradition*, 57; Barry, "Nathaniel Macon," 37. Late in 1794, Macon acknowledged that parties were forming in Congress but eschewed allegiance to either of them. See Kemp P. Battle, ed., *Letters of Nathaniel Macon, John Steele, and William Barry Grove* (Chapel Hill: University of North Carolina Press, 1902), 20-21.

Macon worked closely with Martin Van Buren in Democratic politics during the 1820s and campaigned for his presidenc⁻ in 1836. Van Buren, a Jeffersonian Republican, secretary of state under Andrew Jackson, and eighth president of the United States, supported strict constructionism and states' rights. Portrait of Van Buren, ca. 1840- 862, from the Library of Congress, Washington, D.C.

original states, North Carolina was twelfth to ratify late in 1789. Even after ratification, the state remained wary of national authority.[11]

Almost from the establishment of political structure with Charles II's grant of proprietary control in what would become North Carolina in 1663, the outlines of indigerous dissatisfaction with external rule began to emerge. Once Charleston was established in the 1670s, the Lords Proprietors in England were absorbed by its commercial promise in contrast to the plodding progress of the poorer northern province. Exacerbating the situation was their appointment of a series of weak, if not incompetent, executives for North Carolina as compared to the more capable appointees to the south. When royal control replaced proprietary rule after 1729, the situation improved somewhat, but not enough to overcome a pattern laid down in early years: North Carolina politics was being increasingly dominated by residents and (with the passage of time) natives who controlled the lower house of the assembly, became leaders in the Royal Council, and held sway in the county courts, the most pervasive and effective instruments of government in the colony.

11. Alan D. Watson, "States Rights and Agrarianism Ascendant," in *The Constitution and the States: The Role of the Original Thirteen in the Framing and Adoption of the Federal Constitution*, ed. Patrick T. Conley and John P. Kaminski (Madison, Wis.: Madison House, 1988), 251-267.

Every Crown governor from George Burrington to Josiah Martin bemoaned their conflicts with indigenous alliances of long-resident, often intermarried locals.[12]

Resistance to institutional authority in early North Carolina was not limited to issues of imperial rule versus provincial control. The resident ruling elites who dominated the legislature and court system were in turn often opposed by the poorer classes. The Granville District riots of the 1750s and the Regulator agitation of the 1760s culminating in the Battle of Alamance in 1771 demonstrated a powerful cynicism about and discontent with the growing control of provincial elites.[13] North Carolinians, whether wealthy planters or marginal farmers, had a considerable suspicion of government born of long experience.

The coming of the American Revolution and the constitution-making that followed it underscored North Carolinians' distrust of outside authority. Nathaniel Macon, born in 1758, not only served as a soldier in the fight with Great Britain but also entered politics in the blast furnace of revolution. Elected to the state senate in 1781 while serving in Nathanael Greene's army, Macon took his seat in June and became closely associated with a central figure in determining what the polity of North Carolina would be—Willie Jones.[14]

Macon's native county of Warren (renamed in 1779 for a hero of Bunker Hill) was a cauldron of support for the Patriot cause. His brother Harrison was captured at the Battle of Camden and spent most of the remaining war as a prisoner, and his brother John was a captain in the Continental Line with service at Valley Forge. As early as 1774, the Bute County (from which Warren sprang) Committee of Safety was ready to raise a company "to defend ourselves against any violence," and by June 1775, a total of 114 men were elected to the committee. In February 1778, when an oath of loyalty was administered by the county court before the next election, 604 qualified voters took the oath, and only five refused.[15] In responding to a letter from Archibald Murphey, who was attempting to write a

12. The history of colonial North Carolina is instructively treated in the introductions in Mattie Erma Edwards Parker, William S. Price Jr., and Robert J. Cain, eds., *The Colonial Records of North Carolina* [*Second Series*], volumes 2-9 (Raleigh: Division of Archives and History, North Carolina Department of Cultural Resources, 1968-1988). Other helpful overviews are Hugh T. Lefler and William S. Powell, *Colonial North Carolina: A History* (New York: Charles Scribner's Sons, 1973) and for the royal period, A. Roger Ekirch, *"Poor Carolina": Politics and Society in Colonial North Carolina, 1729-1776* (Chapel Hill: University of North Carolina Press, 1981).

13. The best summary of the many studies of the antecedents and aftermath of the Regulator movement is in H. G. Jones, *North Carolina History: An Annotated Bibliography* (Westport, Conn.: Greenwood Press, 1995), 83-85. Still useful in examining resistance by poor and marginal farmers is Marvin L. Michael Kay, "The North Carolina Regulation, 1766-1776: A Class Conflict" in *The American Revolution: Explorations in the History of American Radicalism*, ed. Alfred F. Young (Dekalb: Northern Illinois University Press, 1976).

14. Barry, "Nathaniel Macon," 10-12.

15. Dodd, *Nathaniel Macon*, 21-28; Norman K. Risjord, *Chesapeake Politics, 1781-1800* (New York: Columbia University Press, 1978), 88; *Bute County Committee of Safety Minutes, 1775-1776* (Warrenton, N.C.: Warren County Bicentennial Committee, 1977), 12, 19-22, 56-64.

history of North Carolina, Nathaniel Macon in 1825 recollected his county's revolutionary past. He mentioned his personal acquaintance with George Sims, a key figure in the Granville District upheavals, and asserted that the Regulation began in adjacent Halifax County. Macon believed that the Bute County Committee of Safety was the first elected in the state and that there were few avowed Loyalists in his county. Such as there were had departed early on.[16]

Having fought in the Revolution, dreaded the uncertainties of postwar disposition of the former Granville District (of which Warren and the other counties in his congressional district had been part), and despised the corruption of English politics, Macon remained proud that his native land had broken with the Mother Country. As late as 1826, he denounced the "rotten boroughs" of Parliament, and at the 1835 state Constitutional Convention in Raleigh, Macon remarked, "He knew most of the men that formed the [North Carolina] Constitution at Halifax in 1776, and that they would have been an ornament to any age. . . . The patriots formed this venerated Constitution and we ought to approach it with awe."[17]

Beginning in 1785, Macon had withdrawn from political life to focus on developing his plantation, Buck Spring. Late in 1783, he had married Hannah Plummer, who bore him two daughters and a son between 1784 and 1787. Not until Hannah's death early in 1790 would Macon resume his political career. Thus, Macon was not an active participant in the roiling arguments surrounding ratification.[18] While absent from the Hillsborough and Fayetteville conventions where the Constitution was debated and finally approved, Macon would certainly have been aware of what was at stake. John Macon was an Antifederalist at the Hillsborough Convention in the summer of 1788, and Nathaniel was allied closely, as were John and Harrison, with Willie Jones of nearby Halifax, the architect of opposition to ratification in Hillsborough and a daunting political force. The three Macon brothers had served together in the legislature in 1782

---

16. Nathaniel Macon to Archibald Murphey, October 15, 1825, Nathaniel Macon Papers, Private Collections, State Archives, hereinafter cited as Macon Papers. Early in 1826, the General Assembly authorized a lottery to raise funds for Murphey's history. The work was never completed. See Charles L. Coon, ed., *The Beginnings of Public Education in North Carolina: A Documentary History, 1790-1840*, 2 vols. (Raleigh, N.C.: Edwards and Broughton, 1908), 1:286.

17. Dodd, *Nathaniel Macon*, 86-87; William K. Boyd, *History of North Carolina*, volume 2: *The Federal Period, 1783-1860* (Chicago: Lewis Publishing Co., 1919), 10-11; *Register of Debates*, 19th Cong., 1st sess., 695; *Proceedings and Debates of the Convention of North-Carolina Called to Amend the Constitution of the State, which Assembled at Raleigh, June 4, 1835* (Raleigh, N.C.: Joseph Gales and Son, 1836), 176-178. Macon opposed congressional appropriations to implement the Jay Treaty early in 1796, largely for fear that it would open the way to lawsuits by the Granville heirs. The Granville District was created by the Crown in 1744 in the northern part of North Carolina as compensation to Earl Granville, who had not sold his proprietary share to the Crown in 1729 as the other seven proprietors had. See William S. Powell, *North Carolina through Four Centuries* (Chapel Hill: University of North Carolina Press, 1989), 86, 93-95.

18. Price, "Nathaniel Macon, Planter," 198; Macon-Eaton Family Bible, Southern Historical Collection, Wilson Library, University of North Carolina at Chapel Hill.

Willie Jones, a Halifax planter and political ally of Macon's, led the opposition to ratification of the Constitution in 1788, when North Carolina delegates gathered to debate the issue in Hillsborough. Portrait of Jones from the State Archives, North Carolina Office of Archives and History, Raleigh.

under Jones's tutelage. He had been the chief author of the Constitution of 1776 and its Declaration of Rights. Friend of Thomas Jefferson and opponent of federal consolidation, Jones was Nathaniel Macon's earliest political mentor.[19]

Nineteenth- and early-twentieth-century views of the Eton-educated, wealthy Jones as "the undisputed leader of the radical party" in North Carolina have always seemed incongruous, and late-twentieth-century historians have rightly challenged them. It is indisputable, however, that Willie Jones was a fervent states' rights advocate. The prospect of a muscular central government—whether in London or, ultimately, Washington—was anathema to him. He declined to attend the Fayetteville Convention in 1789 because of the certainty of ratification and basically withdrew from active politics thereafter.[20]

Because North Carolina was a state where the economy was based on small-scale agriculture, the emphasis on individual rights in Antifederalism would

19. Barry, "Nathaniel Macon," 30; Dodd, *Nathaniel Macon*, 38; Blackwell P. Robinson, *William R. Davie* (Chapel Hill: University of North Carolina Press, 1957), 195-196; Blackwell P. Robinson, "Willie Jones of Halifax," *North Carolina Historical Review* 18 (January and April 1941): 24, 148. John and Nathaniel Macon were among Jones's closest allies. See Dodd, *Nathaniel Macon*, 51.

20. Don Higginbotham, "The Politics of Revolutionary North Carolina: A Preliminary Assessment," in *War and Society in Revolutionary America: The Wider Dimensions of Conflict*, ed. Don Higginbotham (Columbia: University of South Carolina Press, 1988), 67-70; Robinson, "Willie Jones," 161

remain formidable. Without major urban and commercial centers and with numerous religious dissenters in their dispersed population, North Carolinians sought written guarantees of rights and procedures. They were suspicious of assertions not grounded in clear texts. When the state adopted its constitution late in 1776, it first approved a Declaration of Rights before ratification and specifically incorporated those guarantees into the constitutional document. Macon's most recent biographer contends that his strict constructionism sprang from his respect for the written word, whether in a constitution or in Scripture.[21] Nathaniel Macon, younger brother of a proclaimed Antifederalist, protégé of Willie Jones, native and resident of a region and state deeply wary of external rule, thus seemed primed for a political career that would resist the consolidation of governmental power. He would not disappoint.[22]

Entering the U.S. House of Representatives in the Second Congress in October 1791, Macon initially stayed in the background, befitting his status as a novice. He tended to follow the lead of James Madison in voting except when the Virginian would support strong federal authority. By the Third Congress in 1793, however, Macon, along with Federalist William Barry Grove, was senior in the North Carolina delegation, and he became more assertive. Macon would gain notice as a leader in opposing appropriations to carry out the Jay Treaty in 1796.[23]

Throughout a congressional career that spanned thirty-seven years—twenty-four in the House and thirteen in the Senate—as well as in his correspondence

21. William S. Price Jr., " 'There Ought to Be a Bill of Rights': North Carolina Enters a New Nation," in Conley and Kaminski, eds., *The Bill of Rights and the States*, 430-431 (published as a pamphlet by the Office of Archives and History, North Carolina Department of Cultural Resources, in 1991); Michael Lienesch, "North Carolina: Preserving Rights," in *Ratifying the Constitution*, ed. Michael Allen Gillespie and Michael Lienesch (Lawrence: University Press of Kansas, 1989), 362-363; Barry, "Nathaniel Macon," 28. Late in Macon's Senate tenure, he wrote in an undated note: "North Carolina cannot have a large city The adoption of the federal constitution made New York, & destroyed the foreign trade of the southern states." See "Nathaniel Macon in Congress" folder, Katherine Clark Pendleton Conway Collection, Private Collections, State Archives, hereinafter cited as Conway Collection. The many undated notes in this folder appear to have been used by Macon in speeches he made on the floor of Congress Based on the poor quality of his handwriting, all of them seem to date from his Senate service rather than from his long tenure in the House. Surely some of them were used in one of his last important speeches opposing the Tariff of 1828, the so-called Tariff of Abominations. See Elizabeth Gregory McPherson, ed., "Letters from Nathaniel Macon to John Randolph of Roanoke," *North Carolina Historical Review* 39 (April 1962): 204.

22. Although Macon attended the College of New Jersey (later Princeton University), perhaps for as long as two years, the school seems to have made little lasting impact on him. When asked in his later years for advice or advanced schooling, Macon would recommend the College of William and Mary to some and the University of North Carolina to others, but Princeton was conspicuously absent. See Price, "Nathaniel Macon, Planter," 190; Wesley Frank Craven, "Nathaniel Macon," in *Princetonians: A Biographical Dictionary*, volume 3: *1776-1783*, ed. Richard A. Harrison (Princeton, N.J.: Princeton University Press, 1981), 230-236.

23. Barry "Nathaniel Macon," 37-41; Dodd, *Nathaniel Macon*, 56, 86-87. By late 1795, opposition to the Jay Treaty became a party commitment among Republicans. See Elkins and McKitrick, *Age of Federalism*, 441-442.

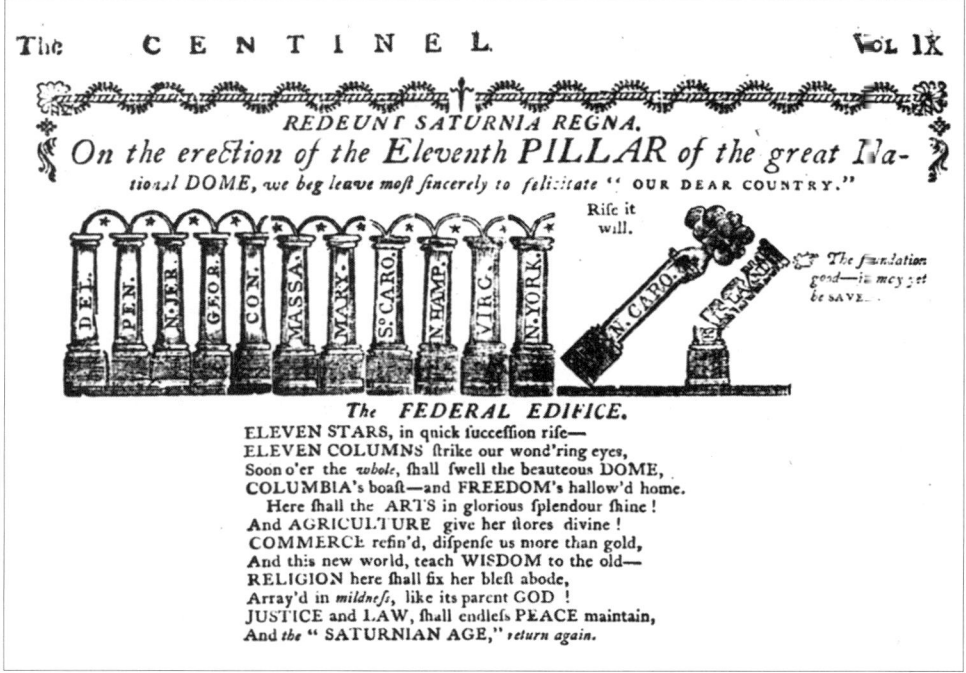

The CENTINEL.   VOL. IX

REDEUNT SATURNIA REGNA.

On the erection of the Eleventh PILLAR of the great National DOME, we beg leave most sincerely to felicitate " OUR DEAR COUNTRY."

Rise it
will.

The foundation
good—is may yet
be SAVE .

The FEDERAL EDIFICE.

ELEVEN STARS, in quick succession rise—
ELEVEN COLUMNS strike our wond'ring eyes,
Soon o'er the whole, shall swell the beauteous DOME,
COLUMBIA's boast—and FREEDOM's hallow'd home.
Here shall the ARTS in glorious splendour shine !
And AGRICULTURE give her stores divine !
COMMERCE refin'd, dispense us more than gold,
And this new world, teach WISDOM to the old—
RELIGION here shall fix her blest abode,
Array'd in mildness, like its parent GOD !
JUSTICE and LAW, shall endless PEACE maintain,
And the " SATURNIAN AGE," return again.

Antifederalists feared that ratifying the federal Constitution of 1787 would concentrate excessive power in the hands of a centralized national authority. The balance of political power, they believed, should lie with individual sovereign states. Of North Carolina, this editorial cartoon notes, "Rise it will." North Carolina was the twelfth state to ratify the Constitution, in November 1789. From the *Massachusetts Centinel*, August 2, 1788. Serial and Government Publications Division, Library of Congress, Washington, D.C.

and public actions after retiring from Washington in 1828, Nathaniel Macon generally evinced his Antifederalist roots in these ways: suspicion of overarching power (especially in the executive branch) and its tendency toward corruption; protection of individual freedoms; support for broad, uncomplicated suffrage for white males exercised in frequent elections; wariness of taxes and patronage; and, above all, insistence on a literal reading of the federal Constitution so as to shield the sovereignty of individual states. A closer examination of Macon's words and actions in each of these five categories is instructive.

Macon's suspicion of power is most clearly expressed in a statement he delivered on the Senate floor in 1816: "ours is a Government of suspicion; every election proves it; the power to impeach proves it; the history of Caesar, of Cromwell, and Bonaparte, proves that it ought to be so to remain free."[24] All three branches of government must maintain a clear separation of powers, lest a single

24. *Annals of Congress*, 14th Cong, 1st sess., 79. Later in the Senate, Macon commented, "All governments, no matter what their form, want more power and authority." See *Annals of Congress*, 16th Cong., 1st sess., 223.

branch become too powerful, he believed. No member of one branch should be able to assume office in another—for example, an incumbent congressman should not be appointed to a cabinet post—and he particularly deplored presidential nominations to the judiciary because they turned into virtual lifetime appointments. If any one of the three branches must have more power than the other two, he avowed, it should be the legislative, elected biennially in the House and chosen by state legislatures in the Senate.[25]

One of the most dreaded potential abuses of power was that of the military. From the start of his congressional career, Macon almost always voted against augmenting the size of the army or navy. He favored militias over standing armies and privateering over a permanent navy.[26] In time of war, a regular army made sense and was less expensive than mobilizing militias, but the United States was not seeking conquest and given its vastness, was best suited to a defensive posture. If invaded, militias and privateers could function ably to repel an enemy as they had done during the Revolution. A regular army and navy afforded too many opportunities for unwarranted expenditures and dangerous ambitions. If the nation wanted to impress potential foes, whether in Algeria, France, England, or elsewhere, then it should formally declare war rather than expand the peacetime military in the hope of generating a threat.[27] In the declared War of 1812, Macon supported expanding the army to fight Great Britain, increasing enlistment terms to five years rather than one, and raising taxes to pay the added expenses. However, he still favored privateering over shipbuilding and opposed conscription as a violation of habeas corpus. Breaking with his close friend John Randolph of Roanoke, who adamantly opposed the war, Macon argued that failure to fight the monarchical British would signal that republican government was unworkable.

25. Edwin Mood Wilson, *The Congressional Career of Nathaniel Macon Followed by Letters of Mr. Macon and Willie P. Mangum with Notes by Kemp P. Battle* (Chapel Hill: University of North Carolina Press, 1900), 65-66; *Proceedings and Debates of the Convention, 1835*, 335-336. During the debates over popular election of the governor in the 1835 state Constitutional Convention, Macon favored maintaining the existing system of legislative selection of the executive. Because the governor lacked a veto—which pleased Macon—his direct election mattered little. It was better for him to remain subservient to the legislature than to make his own appeals to the electorate. See *Proceedings and Debates of the Convention, 1835*, 335-336, 399-400.

26. *Annals of Congress*, 2d Cong., 1st sess., 355; 2d Cong., 2d sess., 802; 3d Cong., 1st sess., 494-497; Elkins and McKitrick, *Age of Federalism*, 595, 717. In May 1794, Macon supported James Madison's position that the Constitution wisely lets the executive direct the military but allows the legislature to authorize and fund it. See *Annals of Congress*, 3d Cong., 1st sess., 709.

27. *Annals of Congress*, 5th Cong., 2d sess., 1671-1674, 1698-1699, 1756-1757; 10th Cong., 1st sess., 1028-1029; Edward R. Cotten, *Life of the Hon. Nathaniel Macon of North Carolina* (Baltimore, Md.: Lucas and Deaver, 1840), 101; Nathaniel Macon to Albert Gallatin, August 2, 1807, Albert Gallatin Papers, New-York Historical Society, New York City (photocopies in State Archives, Raleigh), hereinafter cited as Gallatin Papers; Battle, ed., *Letters of Nathaniel Macon, John Steele, and William Barry Grove*, 82-83; Barry, "Nathaniel Macon," 48, 50, 124-127. Macon wrote early in 1806, "It is not, my friend, easy to raise an army but it is easier to do this than to get clear of one when raised." See Nathaniel Macon to Joseph Nicholson, January 31, 1806, quoted in Barry, "Nathaniel Macon," 127.

Prior to the critical election of 1800, Macon urged Joseph Gales, a congressional journalist, to start a pro-Republican newspaper in North Carolina. In the fall of 1799, Gales issued the first number of the *Raleigh Register*, which regularly attacked Federalist programs and policies. Portrait of Gales by Charles Bird King from the Redwood Library and Athenaeum, Newport, Rhode Island, reproduced by permission.

Still, the Congress must be especially vigilant for any signs of executive expansion or corruption in such stressful times.[28]

Macon also believed in protecting individual freedoms: Although he was not in Congress during the argument for the Bill of Rights, he was subsequently an advocate for it. He was a prominent figure in the debates over the Alien and Sedition Acts in John Adams's presidency and thereby earned the respect of James Madison and other Republicans. During the debates in 1798, Macon argued that the Constitution forbade legislation that would prohibit free speech. The people would assume that any government not allowing unfettered discussion was inherently corrupt. The Sedition Act threatened the press, and the Alien Act challenged the prerogatives of citizens while unduly enhancing executive power.[29]

On the floor of the House in July, Macon argued that if Congress could abridge a free press, then it could establish a religion, as both are from the same part of the Constitution. Members ought to review the ratification debates in the various states, which make clear that no prosecutions for libel by the national government were to occur. Macon believed "the liberty of the press was sacred, and ought to be left where the Constitution had left it. The states have complete power on the

28. Barry, "Nathaniel Macon," 150-156; William K. Boyd, "Nathaniel Macon in National Legislation," *Trinity College Historical Society Papers* (Series 4, 1900), 84.

29. Barry, "Nathaniel Macon," 52-55, 57; Elkins and McKitrick, *Age of Federalism*, 591-59 ; Cornell, *Other Founders*, 231.

subject. . . ." He went on to argue for judicial review should the law pass: "He could only hope that the Judges would exercise the power placed in them of determining the law an unconstitutional law, if, upon scrutiny they find it to be so."[30] Given his strong convictions in these matters, as well as the growing split between Federalists and Democratic-Republicans, Macon urged Joseph Gales to leave his work as a congressional journalist and start a pro-Republican newspaper in North Carolina. In the fall of 1799, Gales issued the first number of the *Raleigh Register* and kept up a steady attack on Federalist programs and policies. His republican loyalties were proven. Gales had been forced to leave his native England in 1795 because of his pro-French views.[31] As he got older, Macon became more critical of the "slanders" and meanspiritedness of the national press, but he rejected censorship. Indeed, at the July 4, 1825, festivities in Warrenton, Macon offered this public toast: "A free press—the Shield of Freedom—the scourge of Tyrants."[32]

Where freedom of religion was concerned, Macon was a strong advocate of separation of church and state and personally tolerant. Although he eschewed church membership, he read the Bible and sometimes attended services at the Baptist meeting near Buck Spring. Macon supported removal of religious tests for officeholding and considered mixing politics and religion "the essence of hypocrisy." No one who reads his correspondence can doubt the reality of his personal religious convictions, but to the end of his life he believed it was wrong for any governmental institution—whether the Congress or a county court—to interfere in matters of conscience.[33]

As to the other kinds of individual freedoms, such as the right of assembly or petition, Macon viewed the best possible government as one that interfered little, if at all with the conduct of ordinary lives. If government did intrude, it ought to be closely monitored. Like his friend Thomas Jefferson, Macon trusted the common sense of the yeomanry over the will of the state. Laws needed to be clear and concise so that citizens could understand their limits as well as their authority. Macon argued, "Every extension of power by construction makes the operation of government more unequal, the [1787] convention aware of this gave but few

30. *Annals of Congress*, 5th Cong., 2d sess., 2105-2106, 2151-2152. Macon continued to speak in support of freedom of the press in the Congress of 1800, even arguing that because it is impossible to draw a line between "freedom of" and "abuse by" the press, it is better for an informed citizenry to make its own judgments than for Congress to interfere. See *Annals of Congress*, 6th Cong., 1st sess., 405-406.

31. Boyd, *History of North Carolina: The Federal Period*, 52; Robinson, *William R. Davie*, 361. Antifederalists viewed an informed citizenry as the key to maintaining liberty. Creating a network of newspapers was crucial to the spread of information. See Cornell, *Other Founders*, 247-248.

32. Nathaniel Macon to Weldon Edwards, April 5, 1828, Macon Papers; *Warrenton Reporter*, July 8, 1825.

33. Price, "Nathaniel Macon, Planter," 205-207. At the 1835 Constitutional Convention, Macon expressed his religious views more completely than anywhere else. He seemed genuinely moved by the pleas of his fellow delegate William Gaston, a Roman Catholic, for removal of the Protestant test oath in the 1776 Constitution.

powers, that convention knew [the] difficulty of managing an unlimited federative Government—a majority may be tyrants."[34]

Macon also advocated wide suffrage for white adult males and frequent elections. He expressed his views, intriguingly, if incompletely, to Jefferson in 1822: "The great principle of American government is election for short periods. . . ." The House of Representatives should be elected by free white males twenty-one or older ("except paupers, lunatics, & those who have committed crime"), and they should be eligible to serve in the House at that age (the Constitution required them to be at least twenty-five). The Senate would be chosen by those thirty years of age or older, although Macon believed that a minimum age of forty might be even better, the object being to have "one branch at an age beyond youthful heat. . . ." Appointments for judges should be abandoned in favor of elections for fixed terms.[35] In earlier times, Macon advocated annual elections for the House, triennial elections for the Senate, and a single eight-year term for the president. At one point he even suggested direct election of the chief executive. He consistently opposed property qualifications for voters. There should be age, residency and tax requirements, but none beyond those. "One house ought to be sufficiently numerous to represent the people fairly, and originate every bill." The other house "should not be numerous but old" and only revise or amend bills.[36]

During debates over moving from annual to biennial legislative elections in the 1835 Constitutional Convention in Raleigh, Macon quoted Jefferson's warning: "Where annual elections end, tyranny begins." A democracy was a government of the people, he added, and should operate on the principles of the American Revolution, among them annual elections. "If you can put off meeting the Legislature for two years, you may extend the time to four, six or ten years. Mr. Jefferson said, he preferred the tempest of Liberty to the calm of Despotism." The principal reason Macon voted against the new constitution in 1835 was its abandonment of annual elections.[37]

---

34. John Lauritz Larson, "Jefferson's Union and the Problem of Internal Improvements," in Jeffersonian Legacies, ed. Peter S. Onuf (Charlottesville: University Press of Virginia, 1993), 345-346; Nathaniel Macon, undated autograph notes, Macon Papers; Price, "Nathaniel Macon, Planter," 212-213; Elkins and McKitrick, Age of Federalism, 760 n. 31.

35. Elizabeth Gregory McPherson, ed., "Unpublished Letters from North Carolinians to Jefferson," North Carolina Historical Review 12 (July and October 1935): 376-377. Macon seems to have written this letter in some haste out of his concerns over the decisions of John Marshall's Supreme Court and following the Missouri Compromise debates. He does not, for instance, specify the frequency of elections nor lengths of terms of office. What is clear, however, is his profound conviction that a broad electorate should be voting often for federal officials.

36. Barry, "Nathaniel Macon," 196-197; Wilson, Congressional Career of Macon Followed by Letters, 65-66.

37. Proceedings and Debates of the Convention, 1835, 91-92, 176-178, 399-400.

This proposed design for the east front of the U.S. Capitol was prepared for Thomas Jefferson in 1806, fifteen years after Macon began his long congressional career (1791-1828). Watercolor and ink on paper by Benjamin H. Latrobe in the Library of Congress.

Finally, in keeping with his principles, Macon refused to participate in the Republican caucuses that nominated presidential candidates after his distasteful experience in the "Marache Club" that nominated Jefferson in 1804. Despite the urgings of various close friends and political allies from Albert Gallatin to Martin Van Buren, Macon believed that the caucus system was too far removed from the people and too subject to deal-making. Unlike his fellow Old Republicans John Taylor of Caroline or John Randolph of Roanoke, Macon eschewed elitism—for example, he never called himself "Nathaniel Macon of Buck Spring"—and embraced the democracy of his day.[38]

Macon was particularly wary of taxes and patronage. The potential abuses of the taxing power and mischievous, even tyrannical, uses of political patronage he found especially odious. They smacked of the liberty-destroying ways of European despotisms. Macon's North Carolina was as averse to taxation as any state and more so than some. That attitude was expressed by an anonymous writer in the *Raleigh Register* on the eve of a legislative session in 1829. In an open letter to the incoming assemblymen, "X" asked why the state needed more roads and canals—could citizens not move from one place to another fairly easily? Support for the university at Chapel Hill was expensive, and "our good old field schools" had met the state's needs well in the past. College-educated people were pretentious, he argued, "and the fewer of them we have amongst us the better. They are antithetical to simple, honest republicanism."[39] While "X" was even more conservative than Macon, his opinions were identical to many of those who venerated Macon and returned him to office term after term.

Taxes weighed heaviest on agrarian, small-scale farmers, in Macon's view. With Jefferson, he saw such people as the bedrock of the country. Massive public works projects seldom reached them or their economic peers in their harscrabble existences. As Macon noted in 1826, "many poor people pay taxes who would not be benefitted [from internal improvements], what advantage would the hunter, the fisherman or the tar burner receive & many others who live on poor land?" He concluded, "The operations of all governments are in favor of the rich . . . every paper system of every kind are for the interest of the rich & cunning, & not for the

---

38. Barry, "Nathaniel Macon," 249-252; Robert Dawidoff, *The Education of John Randolph* (New York: W. W. Norton and Co., 1979), 294; Nathaniel Macon, undated autograph notes, Conway Collection. Macon defined his anti-caucus stance in 1824 in rejecting attendance there in order to support his friend and announced choice, William H. Crawford of Georgia: "No party . . . can last unless found[ed] on pure principles, & the minute a party begins to intrigue within itself is the minute when the seed of dissension is sown & its purity begins to decline." See Nathaniel Macon to Albert Gallatin, February 13, 1824, Gallatin Papers.

39. Coon, ed., *The Beginnings of Public Education in North Carolina*, 1:431-432. Even if "X" should turn out to be a satirist rather than an authentic correspondent (and it is now impossible to know) the views expressed are faithful to those of many North Carolina conservatives of the day.

poor & honest."[40] Growth of public debt assured that taxes must grow too, and the poor and middling citizen would have to work even harder to pay them.[41] Hand in glove with the accumulation of debt and demand for paper currency was the dreaded insistence on a national bank. Macon opposed all measures to charter the Bank of the United States during his congressional career. Of his many negative statements about banks, perhaps the most pointed is this one from 1834: "all banks are alike, because they are nobles of the land & all nobles are alike, have exclusive privileges, which they abuse." Banks sustained an aristocracy of wealth, and the bigger the bank, the more disdainful it was of a democratic people.[42]

Macon abhorred political patronage, especially where a salary or commissions were involved; to him, the whole system resembled despised aspects of British rule. Macon, as a powerful ally of Thomas Jefferson, served as Speaker of the House for the first six of the Virginian's eight years as president and oversaw which North Carolinians would secure federal appointments. Early on he outlined his method: "I shall carefully endeavor to select such as can discharge the duty of office, and have been uniformly democratic, although I do not wish any person turned out of office, who was a whig in the Revolutionary war, for any opinion he may now hold, yet I would not recommend any one for office who had not always been a Republican."[43] Given the rancor of the election of 1800 and the resentment of many about the late appointments of the outgoing Federalist president, John Adams, Macon's statement is hardly that of a rabid party man. In later years he would be even less concerned over partisan loyalty in patronage matters. Fairly typical is this letter to a North Carolinian seeking a federal appointment in 1818: "It is not only proper, but due to you, to state frankly, that it has never been my practice to concern [myself] with appointments, not for the state in which I live, when this shall be known to you, I am sure that you will not desire a change in the practice." Patronage left a bitter taste in Macon's mouth, and despite a persistent regard for Thomas Jefferson, even after he left the White House, Macon increasingly disapproved of the Virginian's use of patronage, especially to woo and

40. Price "Nathaniel Macon, Planter," 212-213; Nathaniel Macon to Bolling Hall, March 18, 1826, Bolling Hall Papers, State Archives, Alabama Department of Archives and History, Montgomery (photocopies in State Archives, Raleigh), hereinafter cited as Hall Papers. His fullest biographer argues that Macon was more egalitarian than most of his political associates and far more trusting of the working classes. See Barry, "Nathaniel Macon," 193-195.

41. Nathaniel Macon to Weldon Edwards, February 17, 1828, Macon Papers; Nathaniel Macon to William H. Crawford, October 13, 1817, William H. Crawford Papers, Rare Book, Manuscript, and Special Collections Library, Duke University, Durham, North Carolina.

42. Nathaniel Macon to Weldon Edwards, May 20, 1834, Weldon N. Edwards Papers, Southern Historical Collection; Barry, "Nathaniel Macon," 185-186; Elizabeth Gregory McPherson, ed., "Unpublished Letters from North Carolinians to Van Buren," *North Carolina Historical Review* 15 (January 1938): 61-62.

43. Wilson, *Congressional Career of Macon Followed by Letters*, 79-81; McPherson, ed., "Letters to Thomas Jefferson" 271-272; *Annals of Congress*, 7th Cong., 1st sess., 713.

reward members of Congress during his second term. Such actions, he believed, undermined the separation of powers essential to good government.[44]

The increasing abuse of patronage was tied to the growth of political parties and their need to reward supporters. The leadership of the Revolutionary generation regarded "party" as an epithet, reeking with the odor of British ministerial corruption. However, by the 1790s, in the tense atmosphere generated in the West by the French Revolution and the British reaction to it, American parties in their modern sense began to evolve. By 1797, Thomas Jefferson was leading, often offstage, the growing opposition to Federalists, whether John Adams or Alexander Hamilton or their allies. Still, the generation that had lived through the American Revolution was uncomfortable with the idea of party while simultaneously aligning with one.[45]

As Jefferson's key supporter in North Carolina, Macon welcomed the growing opposition to Federalist policies, such as hostility to France, loose interpretation of the Constitution, and favor to commercial interests. He delighted in Jefferson's victory in the election of 1800 and was especially buoyed by Republican unity throughout the ordeal of the multiple ballots required to install Jefferson over his vice-president, Aaron Burr. "The election from beginning to end was carried on with great moderation and good humor," Macon wrote.[46] By Jefferson's second term, the political differences between the president as head of the party and Macon as a leader of the Old Republicans—who claimed steadfast allegiance to the Antifederalist principles articulated in the Kentucky and Virginia resolutions of 1798—had deepened. However, Macon never disparaged Jefferson, even after the president failed to support his nomination for a fourth term as Speaker in 1807. Macon, along with John Randolph of Roanoke, considered Jefferson's first term as the high-water mark of Republican practice.[47] Later, in the presidencies of James Madison and James Monroe, Macon saw an erosion of Republican ideals, as these chief executives compromised on measures favoring banks, internal improvements, and tariffs. Macon was never warm to either of them.[48]

44. Nathaniel Macon to "Sir," February 10, 1818, Macon Papers; Barry, "Nathaniel Macon," 100-101.

45. Joseph J. Ellis, *Founding Brothers: The Revolutionary Generation* (New York: Alfred A. Knopf, 2000), 186-187; Elkins and McKitrick, *Age of Federalism*, 484-485, 554-555. John Randolph of Roanoke defined the Old Republican principles well in 1813: "Love of peace, hatred of offensive war, jealousy of State Governments towards the General Government; a dread of standing armies, a loathing of public debt, taxes, and excises; tenderness for the liberty of the citizen; jealousy, Argus-eyed jealousy, of the patronage of the President." Quoted in Kirk, *Randolph of Roanoke*, 89.

46. Nathaniel Macon to "Sir," February 20, 1801, Nathaniel Macon Collection, Library of Congress (photocopies in State Archives, Raleigh).

47. Risjord, *Old Republicans*, 65-66; Dawidoff, *Education of John Randolph*, 172; Thomas Hart Benton, *Thirty Years' View . . . from 1820-1850* (1875; reprint, New York: George Braziller, 1963), 32.

48. Wilson, *Congressional Career of Macon Followed by Letters*, 93-95; McPherson, ed., "Letters to Thomas Jefferson," 378-379; Barry, "Nathaniel Macon," 132.

Macon was closely allied with Thomas Jefferson and was his key supporter in North Carolina. Like Jefferson, he welcomed the growing opposition to Federalist policies, such as hostility to France, loose interpretation of the Constitution, and favor to commercial interests. Portrait of Thomas Jefferson (1805) by Rembrandt Peale, from the New-York Historical Society.

Although Macon supported Andrew Jackson for the presidency in 1828, he waited until late 1827 to endorse him. Macon had known Old Hickory since 1797 and had sizable misgivings about him. He thought that Jackson was headstrong—his unauthorized invasion of Florida in 1818 was particularly worrisome—and while he was a congressman, Jackson had regularly supported internal improvements. Macon endorsed William H. Crawford in the 1824 presidential contest and came to Old Hickory four years later only because he seemed the lesser of two evils, given the re-election hopes of John Quincy Adams. In time, with Jackson's vetoes of the Bank of the United States and the Maysville Road legislation, Macon warmed toward him considerably. Not a little of this enthusiasm sprang from Jackson's increasing reliance on and promotion of Martin Van Buren from secretary of state to vice-president to designated successor.[49]

49. Barry, "Nathaniel Macon," 265-269; Harry L. Watson, *Liberty and Power: The Politics of Jacksonian America* (New York: Noonday Press, 1990), 134-164; Martin Van Buren to supporters in North Carolina, October 4, 1832, Van Buren Papers; Wilson, *Congressional Career of Macon Followed by Letters*, 84-86, 99-100. The Maysville Road bill authorized the federal government to fund the development of a road

Macon also firmly supported strict construction and states' rights. Early in 1799, Jefferson offered this statement, which Macon welcomed: "I am for preserving to the States the powers not yielded by them to the Union, and to the legislature of the Union its constitutional share of the division of powers; I am not for transferring all the powers of the States to the general government and all those of that government to the Executive branch." The federal government possessed only those powers specifically delineated in the Constitution—beyond that literal reading lurked the fearful potential for abuse of power, especially by an ambitious executive.[50]

From early in his congressional career, Macon made his own strict constructionist views clear. The states would never have approved the Constitution—and underscored their views in the Tenth Amendment—if it meant surrendering sovereignty within their borders. Furthermore, the nation owed its creation to the states. Macon even noted that state legislatures could render the federal government impotent by refusing to elect senators to Congress, thereby paralyzing the political process.[51]

As early as George Washington's presidency, Macon disagreed with those who sought to broaden federal powers through a liberal interpretation of the Constitution. As time progressed, that loose reading of parts of the fundamental law would only expand. By 1818, Macon was warning a fellow Republican who was drawn to Henry Clay's program of internal improvements: "If Congress can make canals, they can with more propriety emancipate. Be not deceived I speak soberly in the fear of God, and the love of the Constitution, Let not love of improvement, or a thirst for glory blind that sober discretion and sound sense with which the Lord has blest you . . . add not to the Constitution nor take therefrom." Seven years later, in repeating these arguments to the same correspondent, Macon would add that during the ratification debates, "the authors of the book, now called the federalist" made no claim of federal power to authorize banks, roads, or canals.[52]

---

from Maysville to Lexington, Kentucky. Jackson objected on the grounds that the project would only benefit Kentucky and was not in the national interest.

50. Thomas Jefferson to Elbridge Gerry, January 26, 1799, quoted in Barry, "Nathaniel Macon," 65; Risjord, *Old Republicans*, 1. Given his strict constructionism, Jefferson was concerned about the constitutionality of the Louisiana Purchase in 1803 and considered seeking an amendment to permit "enlargement of the Union." However, Secretary of the Treasury Albert Gallatin argued that the United States had an inherent right as a sovereign nation to acquire territory, and Macon seems to have shared his view. See Dumas Malone, *Jefferson the President: First Term, 1801-1805* (Boston: Little, Brown and Co., 1970), 311-332.

51. *Annals of Congress*, 5th Cong., 2d sess., 2151-2152; Barry, "Nathaniel Macon," 55-56.

52. Wilson, *Congressional Career of Macon Followed by Letters*, 46-50, 76-78. For Macon's views of slavery, see Price, "Nathaniel Macon, Planter," 201-204.

The Founding Fathers had wisely provided an amending procedure for the Constitution, and that was the route Macon commended if change were necessary. Late in 1810, he himself proposed an amendment that would prohibit congressmen from accepting executive branch appointments during a presidential term in which they had sat in the legislature. It failed, but Macon's dogged insistence on a clear separation of powers as well as his distaste for patronage manipulation was underscored. On the Senate floor in 1826, he rejected the notion that the Constitution was "too sacred" to be amended, as one member had suggested. To be sure, amendments should neither be frivolous nor frequent, he believed, but the Congress was obliged to remedy serious wrongs. Above all, one should rely on the wisdom of the voters: "This Government is founded on the principle that the People have sense enough to govern themselves; and if passion should sometimes show itself, it will burn out, and reason will resume her throne, and the thing will come right."[53] This statement, coming two months before the death of Jefferson, would have pleased him.

The aftermath of the War of 1812 saw a national growth in commercial development that fueled a push for internal improvements, banks, a bigger navy, and other federal expenditures. The competition among politicians to claim a share of these appropriations for their constituencies increased the lure of loose construction, of an easier way to spend federal money widely. In 1828, Macon lamented, "The Constitution is out of fashion, you know it was buried, but the funeral discourse never published, so that its death, was not generally heard of, before fashion laid it by." Near the end of his congressional career, he made the same point in a debate on funding the Chesapeake and Ohio Canal—that the Constitution did not specifically authorize internal improvements was simply no longer a concern of most members; they brushed that question aside without a second thought.[54] After Macon retired from the national stage, his stance on internal improvements only hardened. At the 1835 Constitutional Convention, he opposed any governmental role in them whatsoever. Such improvements were best undertaken by the private sector, where cheaper rates could be leveraged.[55]

Macon not only believed the Constitution should be literally interpreted in the matter of public works, but he also deeply dreaded the ways in which such projects could breed corruption. As he said in 1821 in opposing the Ohio-Erie

53. *Register of Debates*, 19th Cong., 1st sess., 695-696; Barry, "Nathaniel Macon," 145-146, 188.

54. Nathaniel Macon to Weldon Edwards, February 22, 1828, Macon Papers.

55. *Proceedings and Debates of the Convention, 1835*, 91-92. That Southern concerns over nationally funded internal improvements continued beyond the 1835 Constitutional Convention is witnessed by their prohibition in article 1, section 8 (3) of the Constitution of the Confederacy. The Confederate drafters were much influenced by Antifederalist writings. See Marshall L. DeRosa, *The Confederate Constitution of 1861: An Inquiry into American Constitutionalism* (Columbia: University of Missouri Press, 1991), 57-65, 120-134.

Canal, government funding "would encourage a spirit of speculation among the people, which it is the duty of Government to discountenance." When money became the standard for judging personal worth, social morality suffered.[56]

It is instructive to examine Macon's stance on two questions of huge national significance, one occurring while he was in Congress, the other after his retirement—the Missouri Compromise in 1820 and the Nullification Crisis a dozen years later. In each case, his positions on strict construction and states' rights are forthrightly expounded.

The question of admitting Missouri as a state late in 1819 touched off a series of ringing debates between those seeking to prevent the spread of slavery and those advocating its extension. The short-term issue was how Missouri's admission as a state in which slavery would be legal might disturb the delicate balance of free and slave states in the Senate. Early in 1820, Macon rose in that body to deliver his most passionate speech since calling for war with England in 1812. He rejected the claims of some members that the Declaration of Independence, in which "all men are created equal," was part of the Constitution and argued that slavery was in fact a positive good—that it benefited both former Africans and white society.[57] Macon argued that if Congress could restrict slave ownership in Missouri, it might likewise abolish the practice in other sovereign states. There was no constitutional authority for Congress to do either, in his view. Suppose universal emancipation occurred, Macon asked. What might result? A situation like the one in which Revolutionary France freed the slaves of Santo Domingo three decades earlier and opened the way to violence and chaos? Could the present Constitution survive? Macon feared it would not: "Because the rich would, in such circumstances want titles and hereditary distinctions; the negro food and raiment; and they [the emancipated] would be as much or more degraded, than in their present condition. The rich might hire those wretched people, and with them attempt to change this Government. . . ."[58]

After he retired from the Senate in 1828, numerous politicians still sought Macon's opinions, knowing in what high regard he was held not only in his native state, but also throughout the South. During the Nullification Crisis of the early

---

56. *Annals of Congress*, 16th Cong., 2d sess., 144; Price, "Nathaniel Macon, Planter," 212. Like Albert Gallatin, Macon believed that public debt fueled speculation, that speculators consumed extravagantly in order to spend more, and that their luxury was based in financial manipulation rather than productive investment. In Macon's view, extravagance inevitably fostered corruption. See Cornell, *Other Founders*, 179-180.

57. Barry, "Nathaniel Macon," 219-222; Risjord, *Old Republicans*, 215.

58. *Annals of Congress*, 16th Cong., 1st sess., 225; Price, "Nathaniel Macon, Planter," 202. In February 1820, Macon suggested to a friend in Alabama that he should follow the Missouri debates because all other matters before Congress paled in comparison. He recommended the *National Intelligencer* (Washington, D.C.) newspaper as the best source of information. See Nathaniel Macon to Bolling Hall, February 13, 1820, Hall Papers.

1830s, from the White House, both Andrew Jackson and Martin Van Buren sought the ex-senator's views. South Carolina, led by John C. Calhoun, was arguing that it had the sovereign authority to reject federal laws it deemed harmful, such as the tariffs of 1828 and 1832. President Jackson disagreed and was prepared to use military force, if necessary, to enforce national authority. Where would a strict constructionist and states' rights advocate like Macon stand?[59]

Macon made it clear that he was no nullifier; he told Van Buren, "I am still for the union. . . ." About the same time, he wrote to a former congressman: "To nullify & be in the union seems to be impossible." States could not reject a federal law just because it was detestable to them. What was the only remedy for a state then? Secession.[60] As he told Van Buren, "The right to quit, is the best and almost only guard against oppression." Macon held that in order to secede, a state would be obliged to pay its part of the public debt and to accept that future readmission would require the approval of all the other states, but without the right of withdrawal, a state could become like unhappy Ireland under Great Britain.[61]

For his part, President Jackson undertook a profound exchange of letters with Macon in the throes of the crisis. When Old Hickory reminded Macon that he and Jefferson had backed the constitutionally suspect embargo in 1808, the ex-congressman replied: "Mr. Jefferson and myself may have done wrong, in the very hot times, in which we acted; I, however, never approved of construing the Constitution by precedent." Macon rejected the extreme states' rights argument of nullifiers but spoke again of the right of secession. He disliked Jackson's Force Bill, which granted the chief executive authority to employ the military to enforce federal law, and said that if conquered, South Carolina would be "a foreign country." The states and the Union could not be kept together by force but only by mutual regard and interest. Jackson regarded secession as treasonable, and neither he nor Macon ever relented in their stands. That a strong-willed president would go to such lengths to argue his position with a leading, albeit retired, Old Republican underscores Macon's enduring stature among so many Democratic-Republicans. No longer on the national stage in Washington, Macon nevertheless remained a palpable link to certain aspects of the American Revolution and to Antifederalism. Jacksonian Democrats valued that linkage.[62]

59. Barry, "Nathaniel Macon," 284-288.

60. McPherson, ed., "Letters to Van Buren," 59; Nathaniel Macon to Bolling Hall, April 14, 1833, Hall Papers.

61. McPherson, ed., "Letters to Van Buren," 59; Wilson, *Congressional Career of Macon Followed by Letters*, 63-65.

62. Wilson, *Congressional Career of Macon Followed by Letters*, 61-65; Barry, "Nathaniel Macon," vi, 284-287. One scholar notes that while Old Republicans such as Macon and Randolph feared emancipation, they never made the defense of slavery a central political concern as Calhoun and others did. With the exception of the Force Bill, Macon and Randolph were generally strong supporters of

After his election to the House of Representatives in 1795, Albert Gallatin became a member of the finance committee and joined the Republican Party. An ally of Nathaniel Macon, Gallatin opposed expansion of the military and the Alien and Sedition Acts. He later served as secretary of the treasury under Jefferson and Madison. Portrait of Gallatin from *Dictionary of American Portraits*, 230.

That Macon gained so much respect during his long congressional career was due more to his practical sense and his steadfast dependability than to his political genius. Intellectually, he was no Jefferson, Gallatin, or Calhoun. What he did bring to the political arena, however, was an overall consistency of thought and action that set him apart from the jockeying for advantage that marked too many of his colleagues. Macon's unstinting support of his mercurial, often acerbic colleague John Randolph of Roanoke for chairmanship of the powerful Ways and Means Committee in the House probably precluded his getting a fourth term as Speaker. His refusal after 1804 to participate in the caucus system for choosing presidential candidates disappointed such good and powerful friends as Gallatin, Crawford, Van Buren, and others. That he voted on the losing side against his state's constitution of 1835, after presiding over the convention that wrote it, fitted the overall pattern of his career. In this instance, Macon reckoned that the new constitution increased the executive power while removing the legislature further from the electorate. For one who cut his teeth on Antifederalism, that was anathema.[63]

Macon took great pride in refusing to seek preferment. In an undated autograph note after leaving the Senate, he wrote, "I never solicited any man to vote for me, or hinted to him, that I wished him to do so, nor did I ever solicit any person to make interest for me, to be elected to any place." His close friend and protégé, Weldon Edwards, confirmed as much in his brief biography of Macon and added that once a year Macon would attend the first day of court in each county in his district, where he met with constituents and answered their questions. Beyond that congenial outreach, there was nothing that could be construed as "campaigning."[64]

Macon believed in a democratic localism where voters could know and watch their elected representatives. Surely his most notable heir in embracing the ideal of democratic localism was Martin Van Buren. For Van Buren, the key to understanding American political culture was to recognize and appreciate its decentralized character. Suspicion of a strong national state was a cardinal principle of Antifederalism, and Van Buren knew that recognizing the role of such wariness among the public was essential to comprehending the "mind of America." His old friend Nathaniel Macon might not have articulated that view so clearly as Van Buren, but he surely would have nodded his assent. Distrust of a remote, manipulative central authority is not only a part of the legacy of Antifederalism to both Nathaniel Macon and Martin Van Buren, but also to the political left and right in modern America as well.[65]

63. Barry "Nathaniel Macon," 237; Boyd, *History of North Carolina: The Federal Period*, 56-57; William E. Dodd, "The Place of Nathaniel Macon in Southern History," *American Historical Review* 7 (July 1902): 667-668; Price, "Nathaniel Macon, Planter," 210.

64. Nathaniel Macon, undated autograph note, Nathaniel Macon Manuscripts, Duke Special Collections; Weldon N. Edwards, *Memoir of Nathaniel Macon, of North Carolina* (Raleigh, N.C.: *Raleigh Register* Steam Power Press, 1862), 11-12.

65. Cornell, *Other Founders*, 298-305.

Nathaniel Macon, Planter

W hen the convention to consider changing the constitution of North Carolina convened in Raleigh in June 1835, the delegates gathered from every corner of the state unanimously chose as presiding officer the most venerated man among them: Nathaniel Macon of Warren County. The seventy-six-year-old Macon, thrice Speaker of the U.S. House of Representatives and later U.S. senator, had returned to his native state since retiring from the national arena in 1828 As had been the case with every elective office he had held throughout a political career that began in 1781, Macon had not sought presidency of the convention, but he willingly accepted it. He asked the delegates to be patient with him since he had become "rusty" regarding rules of procedure during his retirement. Surprisingly vocal during the convention, Macon offered many comments that were recorded by Weston R. Gales, the official reporter of the proceedings. In one of those statements, Macon defined himself as a "planter." Gales reported on June 15 of Macon: "The term Farmer, he said, was seldom heard in North Carolina, and he was glad of it, as it always indicated to him a state of tenantry—he preferred the term *Planter*, which conveyed to his mind more of independence and plenty."[1]

Nathaniel Macon was a planter's son. His own plantation, Buck Spring in northeastern Warren County, was a devise from his father, Gideon Hunt Macon. Gideon had migrated from his native Virginia to the Shocco Creek area of what would become Bute County and later Warren. He settled there about 1737 on the "southside of the Roanoke" (the area between the Roanoke and Neuse Rivers west of Tarborough) as did another Virginian, Philemon Hawkins. By 1760, Gideon had eight children with his wife, Priscilla Jones, and was one of the wealthiest men in the county. He was then about forty-five years old.[2] Gideon Macon would not live to be forty-seven. Priscilla acted as executrix when his will was probated in

1. *Proceedings and Debates of the Convention of North-Carolina Called to Amend the Constitution of the State, which Assembled at Raleigh, June 4, 1835* (Raleigh, N.C.: Joseph Gales and Son, 1836), 91-92; *Raleigh Register*, June 9, 1835. The best-known biography of Macon and one that is still useful is William E. Dodd, *The Life of Nathaniel Macon* (Raleigh, N.C.: Edwards and Broughton, 1903). A recent doctoral dissertation is the most useful biography of Macon to date. See Stephen J. Barry, "Nathaniel Macon: The Prophet of Pure Republicanism, 1758-1837" (Ph.D. diss., State University of New York at Buffalo, 1995).

2. Barry, "Nathaniel Macon," 2-3; William E. Dodd, "The Place of Nathaniel Macon in Southern History," *American Historical Review* 7 (July 1902): 663.

February 1762. Young Nathaniel, not yet four years old, would receive five hundred acres about fifteen miles north of Macon Manor "lying on both sides of Hubquarter Creek." Shortly after his twenty-first birthday in 1779, he took up residence there and called the place "Buck Spring." It would be home for the rest of his life.[3]

Opportunities for formal schooling for most young gentry in the early South were quite limited, in North Carolina especially. Many planters hired a tutor who would reside right on the plantation. In 1766, Priscilla Macon agreed with her neighbor Philemon Hawkins to engage a tutor to teach her sons John and Nathaniel and his, Joseph and Benjamin. The twenty-two-year-old man they hired was Charles Pettigrew. Pettigrew would reside with the Hawkinses on their plantation three miles north of Bute County Courthouse. Instruction was conducted in the courthouse five miles away from Macon Manor to the south—thus nearly halfway between the two families.[4]

The choice of Pettigrew was a solid one. Born in Pennsylvania in 1744, young Charles moved with his family to Virginia ten years later and in about 1760 to Granville County, North Carolina. Raised in a strict Presbyterian family, Charles had been schooled in a classical academy in Virginia and then in 1763 began studies with the Reverend Henry Pattillo in North Carolina. Pettigrew had been immersed in classical Greek and Roman writers during his Virginia days, and in Pattillo he encountered a master grammarian. Pettigrew's own teaching would center on exercises in Greek and Latin writers.[5] Young Nathaniel Macon was much influenced by his teacher, who would advance to greater renown after leaving Bute in 1773 to become master of the academy at Edenton. Ultimately, Pettigrew (who became an Anglican in 1774) would be first Episcopal bishop-elect of North Carolina.[6]

A glance at the writings of Pettigrew and his mentor, Henry Pattillo, resonates with the kinds of rhythms that would resound throughout Macon's life. Pattillo in 1787 advised his readers to avoid "the temptation of riches; and avoid debts and foreign frippery . . . to pay your public and private debts *is rendering to God the glory*

3. Boyd L. Cathey, "Nathaniel Macon and Buck Spring" (report, Research Branch, Division of Archives and History, Raleigh, 1975), Nathaniel Macon Section (this report does not have numbered pages); Shawn Bonath, "Buck Spring: Archaeology of an Old South Plantation" (report, Research Branch, Division of Archives and History, Raleigh, 1978), 1-2.

4. Richard M. Weaver, *The Southern Tradition at Bay: A History of Postbellum Thought* (1968; reprint, Washington, D.C.: Regnery Gateway, 1989), 56-65; Merritt Bloodworth Pound, "Colonel Benjamin Hawkins, North Carolinian, Benefactor of the Southern Indians," parts 1 and 2, *North Carolina Historical Review* 19 (January/April 1942): 1-3; Dodd, *Life of Nathaniel Macon*, 4-7.

5. Sarah McCulloh Lemmon, *Parson Pettigrew of the "Old Church," 1744-1807* (Chapel Hill: University of North Carolina Press, 1970), 4-8. In 1770, Pettigrew purchased volumes by Terence, Juvenal, Cicero, and Ovid for use in his Bute classroom.

6. Sarah McCulloh Lemmon, ed., *The Pettigrew Papers*, 2 vols. to date (Raleigh: Division of Archives and History, Department of Cultural Resources, 1971-), 1:x.

Warren County plantation owner Nathaniel Macon (1758-1837) was thrice elected Speaker of the U.S. House of Representatives, served as U.S. senator for thirteen years, and presided over the 1835 state constitutional convention. Macon, who ardently supported Republican principles of individual freedom and a limited federal government, considered himself a "planter," a term that conveyed to him a sense of "independence and plenty." Robert D. Gauley portrait of Nathaniel Macon courtesy of the Architect of the Capitol, Washington, D.C. The painting is located in the Speakers Lobby and is part of the U.S. House of Representatives collection.

due unto his name—That to cultivate your field is to *work out your own salvation*—That to fill your barns with plenty is to *lay up treasure in heaven. . . .*" Writing to his sons in 1797, Pettigrew cautioned them never to be overly confident and to be honest and truthful in all of their dealings. "The world is envious and ill-natured," he wrote. He enjoined his slave-owning sons to remember about their slaves: "They are slaves for life. They are not stimulated to care and industry as white people are, who labor for themselves. They do not feel interested in what they do, for arbitrary masters and mistresses; and their education is not such as can be expected to inspire them to sentiments of honor and gratitude."[7] Macon's adult attitudes toward his plantation, his slaves, his personal conduct, indeed, toward the government of his state and nation bore the marks of his teachers. To read his letters or speeches in Congress is to hear the lessons of Pattillo and Pettigrew many times over.

In 1774, young Macon followed his two Hawkins schoolmates and his brother to the Presbyterian-affiliated College of New Jersey (later Princeton University). The curriculum there was dominated by studies in Greek, Latin, mathematics, French, and theology. Macon never completed his Princeton studies. In mid-1776, the faculty and students of the college dispersed at news of a British invasion. Nathaniel joined a local militia company and served a tour of duty on the Delaware. He may have returned briefly to Princeton but was back home by 1777. Three years later Macon was again in the patriot army as British forces concentrated on the South. He fought in the Battle of Camden and may have fought at Guilford Courthouse before taking a seat in the North Carolina Senate in 1781.[8]

That his former teacher would keep up with his Bute Courthouse students is attested to by this 1802 letter of Charles Pettigrew to Benjamin Hawkins: "Sir, the prosperity and respectability of any of my old pupils gives me the sincerest pleasure, and I am particularly pleased to find that your old schoolmate Macon makes so respectable a figure in Congress."[9] Pettigrew likewise would have been pleased that Macon remained a reader of the Bible and Greek, Roman, and English history throughout his life. Macon was fond of telling young visitors to Buck Spring that no one ever surpassed Homer in poetry, Demosthenes in oratory, Samson in strength, and Solomon in wisdom.[10]

In an 1814 letter to a young kinsman who had requested advice on schooling, Macon wrote, "while you are young make yourself acquainted with the history of England. . . . next to being acquainted with the history of our own country, we ought to be acquainted with the history of that, because our laws and customs are in very great measure derived from her." Further on he said, "read the histories of Greece & Rome, and not to forget the Bible & testament, with them everyone

7. Quoted in Robert M. Calhoon, ed., "An Agrarian and Evangelical Culture," in *The North Carolina Experience: An Interpretive and Documentary History*, ed. Lindley S. Butler and Alan D. Watson (Chapel Hill: University of North Carolina Press, 1984), 180-183. Henry Pattillo was chairman of the Bute County Committee of Safety at the start of the American Revolution. See *Bute County Committee of Safety Minutes, 1775-1776* (Warrenton, N.C.: Warren County Bicentennial Committee, 1977), 2, 12.

8. Undated manuscript in Macon's hand in Nathaniel Macon Manuscripts, Rare Book, Manuscript, and Special Collections, Perkins Library, Duke University, Durham, North Carolina; C. L. Grant, ed., *Letters, Journals, and Writings of Benjamin Hawkins*, 2 vols. (Savannah, Ga.: Beehive Press, 1980), 1:ix; Barry, "Nathaniel Macon," 5-6. Four of Macon's biographers (Edward Cotten, Weldon Edwards, Dodd, and Barry) have slightly differing accounts of how long he was at Princeton and when he returned to North Carolina. They also differ on his Revolutionary war service. Dodd and Barry are most reliable, and Barry is best on Macon's military record. See Barry, "Nathaniel Macon," 5-11.

9. Lemmon, *Pettigrew Papers*, 1:295-296.

10. Edward R. Cotten, *Life of Hon. Nathaniel Macon of North Carolina* (Baltimore: Lucas and Deaver, 1840), 258, 261.

ought to be well acquainted." He closed with this practical suggestion: "A very good plan to improve yourself, would be to read a paper in the Spectator or Guardian, and then write as near like it, as you can, after writing compare yours and the original together, this is the plan which Dr. [Benjamin] Franklin when young adopted to improve himself and his style and no one has written in a more easy and elegant style than the Doctor."[11]

Macon preferred the College of William and Mary (alma mater of his friends Thomas Jefferson and John Randolph of Roanoke) over any other in the nation. In 1835, he said that it had produced "more celebrated men than any other college," in part due to its location in Williamsburg—a community with a busy political and social environment. He went on to suggest that the University of North Carolina (UNC) would be improved by moving from bucolic Chapel Hill to the more vibrant seat of government, Raleigh, because "the manners of boys should be attended to as well as their minds." Through education, Macon maintained, North Carolinians could "become a virtuous, if not a great people."[12] Macon served for a long period as a trustee at UNC. His brother John was an original trustee of the university, as was Nathaniel's political mentor, Willie Jones. Indeed, the Antifederalist Jones and his Federalist nephew-in-law, William R. Davie, were from the earliest days of statehood persistent advocates of a public university.[13] Macon's views on education were consistent with those of an entire generation of Revolutionary leaders in the South, if not of the nation as a whole. Most members of that elite southern generation, like Macon, were planters.[14]

The native country and lifelong home of Nathaniel Macon was one of the richest agricultural regions of North Carolina and the South. Watered by the Roanoke River, its farms produced abundant crops and livestock.[15] The river

11. Nathaniel Macon to Francis A. Thornton, October 20, 1814, Nathaniel Macon Papers, Private Collections, State Archives, North Carolina Office of Archives and History, Raleigh, hereinafter cited as Macon Papers. The erratic punctuation and capitalization are Macon's own and are not unique to his generation of Americans. See James Marvin Helms, "The Early Career of Nathaniel Macon: A Study in Pure Republicanism" (Ph.D. diss., University of Virginia, 1962), 8.

12. *Proceedings and Debates of the Convention, 1835*, 43. In 1826, Macon had written, "Had a son, he would not be sent to a college north of Virginia." Nathaniel Macon to Bolling Hall, March 18, 1826, Bolling Hall Papers, State Archives, Alabama Department of Archives and History, Montgomery (photocopies in State Archives, Raleigh), hereinafter cited as Hall Papers. For Nathaniel Macon's long career of service to the University of North Carolina, see Barry, "Nathaniel Macon," 276.

13. Blackwell P. Robinson, *William R. Davie* (Chapel Hill: University of North Carolina Press, 1957), 225, 267. Don Higginbotham rightly questions how "radical" a leader Jones was prior to 1787 when young Macon was first coming to know him. See Don Higginbotham, "The Politics of Revolutionary North Carolina: A Preliminary Assessment," in *War and Politics in Revolutionary America: The Wider Dimensions of the Conflict*, ed. Don Higginbotham (Columbia: University of South Carolina Press, 1988) 69-70.

14. Jackson Turner Main, *The Social Structure of Revolutionary America* (Princeton, N.J.: Princeton University Press, 1965), 50-67. Southern planters believed that education beyond the primary level was solely for members of their social class. Higher education carried a mandate for public service. See Weaver, *The Southern Tradition at Bay*, 56-63.

15. Johann David Schoepf, *Travels in the Confederation, 1783-1784*, trans. Alfred J. Morrison, 2 vols. (Philadelphia: William J. Campbell, 1911), 2:121; Elkanah Watson, *Men and Times of the Revolution*, ed.

began in the mountains west of Roanoke, Virginia, and fell four hundred miles to the Albemarle Sound. The flat valley that it passed through in North Carolina was chiefly in Halifax, Bertie, Northampton, and Warren Counties (in descending order of affected acreage). Before the river was harnessed by a dam in the 1950s, it often flooded. Those floods produced some of the richest soil in America.[16] Nathaniel Macon's Buck Spring was less than four miles from the Roanoke River.[17]

The social and commercial centers of Macon's country were the towns of Halifax and Warrenton. Although Buck Spring was twelve miles from Warrenton and twice that far from Halifax, Macon's public and private life were linked to the towns both politically and culturally.[18] In 1767, the population of Halifax County was 8,755 (6,210 white and 2,545 black) and of Bute County (from which Warren and Franklin Counties were formed in 1779), 7,104 (5,326 white and 1,778 black). Only the Lower Cape Fear Valley had a greater density in pre-Revolutionary North Carolina. By 1776, the proportion of slaves living on large plantations in the Roanoke Valley was comparable to the distributive patterns in Tidewater Virginia and Maryland.[19] Macon's country was thus linked to the larger "world" of the Chesapeake region via Halifax County and the slightly smaller and less grand places of the eastern Piedmont via Warren.[20] Throughout his life,

Winslow C. Watson (New York: Dana and Co., 1856), 58; J. F. D. Smyth, A Tour in the United States of America, 2 vols. (Dublin: T. Henshall, 1784), 1:57; Norman K. Risjord, Chesapeake Politics, 1781-1800 (New York: Columbia University Press, 1978), 55-56. In 1954, Caledonia State Prison Farm in Halifax County produced more corn, beef, pork, and potatoes by far than any other farm in the state's prison system. See Bill Sharpe, A New Geography of North Carolina, 4 vols. (Raleigh, N.C.: Sharpe Publishing Co., 1954), 1:152.

16. Elizabeth W. Wilborn, Boyd D. Cathey, and Jerry L. Cross, "The Roanoke Valley: A Report for the Historic Halifax State Historic Site" (report, Research Branch, Division of Archives and History, Raleigh, 1974), Part I, B (this report does not have numbered pages); Jane Turner Censer, North Carolina Planters and their Children, 1800-1860 (Baton Rouge: Louisiana State University Press, 1984), 1; Cornelius Oliver Cathey, Agricultural Developments in North Carolina, 1783-1860 (Chapel Hill: University of North Carolina Press, 1956), 53.

17. B. Cathey, "Nathaniel Macon and Buck Spring," Nathaniel Macon and Buck Spring Section.

18. Wilborn, Cathey, and Cross, "The Roanoke Valley," Part I, G; Manly Wade Wellman, The County of Warren, North Carolina, 1586-1917 (Chapel Hill: University of North Carolina Press, 1959), 70.

19. Marvin L. Michael Kay and Lorin Lee Cary, "A Demographic Analysis of Colonial North Carolina with Special Emphasis upon the Slave and Black Populations," in Black Americans in North Carolina and the South, ed. Jeffrey J. Crow and Flora J. Hatley (Chapel Hill: University of North Carolina Press, 1984), 77, 82-83, 88; Marvin L. Michael Kay and Lorin Lee Cary, Slavery in North Carolina, 1748-1775 (Chapel Hill: University of North Carolina Press, 1995), 24. The Northern Inner Plain Piedmont (Halifax, Edgecombe, Bute, Granville, and Northampton Counties) had a free black population comprising 6.77 percent of the total black population in 1767; the Lower Cape Fear region, only 1.06 percent. The average free black population for the entire state was 5.35 percent of the total black population.

20. Risjord, Chesapeake Politics, 48-51; Robinson, William R. Davie, 150; Robert Dawidoff, The Education of John Randolph (New York: W. W. Norton and Co., 1979), 34-35. Cultural distinctions between the towns of Halifax and Warrenton were slight, although Halifax was more of a commercial center. Where their respective counties were concerned though, Halifax was the western limit of the northern Coastal Plain, and Warren was the eastern limit of the northern Piedmont. Buck Spring was on the border of the two regions.

Antifederalist Willie Jones, Macon's political mentor and one of the largest slaveholders in the state, served in the North Carolina Senate (1782, 1784, 1788), House of Commons (1777-1780), and the Continental Congress (1780). Both Jones and Macon were trustees of the University of North Carolina. Jones's plantation, "The Grove," pictured here in a drawing by Edwin Hodgkin, was built on the Halifax side of the Roanoke River and became a social and political center among the northeastern North Carolina planter elite. Copy courtesy of the State Archives, North Carolina Office of Archives and History, Raleigh.

Macon would evince elements of Chesapeake sophistication and Piedmont rusticity. He surely was more emotionally attached to the latter, but to think that he spurned the former is to fail to comprehend him.

On the eve of the American Revolution, the banks of the Roanoke River in North Carolina were dotted with warehouses storing goods for shipment to markets. The port town of Halifax then had about fifty houses and three taverns in addition to several warehouses. Since 1758, public warehouses in the town were authorized to inspect tobacco bound for market. Prior to that, farmers in the area went to Virginia for such inspections. Hogsheads of tobacco, wheat, and other agricultural products as well as large quantities of lumber were loaded onto piraguas, flatboats, and even two-masted sloops to travel the sixty miles downriver to Edenton and the Albemarle Sound. The town of Halifax was the upper limit of the Roanoke for vessels able to transport up to two hundred hogsheads, and thus it became the nearest hub of market access for many farms in upper North Carolina.[21]

Further enhancing the commercial advantages of Halifax were biennial fairs (first authorized by the General Assembly in 1777) for the sale of horses, cattle, sheep, hogs, tobacco, and merchandise. Newspaper advertisements in 1792 include those for hairdressers, tailors, clockmakers, booksellers, slave auctions, and thoroughbred horse sales.[22] Visitor J. F. D. Smyth in late-eighteenth-century Halifax observed woolens, linens, shoes, books, hats, liquor, and sugar being imported and tobacco, skins, furs, cotton, butter, and flour as exports. By 1786, Halifax County was the most populous in the state with 10,327 people and a black majority (50.7 percent).[23] Also in 1786, Halifax hosted a three-day cockfighting match with rival birds from Virginia, and hundreds of spectators crowded the town for the event. By 1793, horse races were regularly staged in the town each spring and fall. Indeed, cockfighting and horse racing would become near-obsessions of Roanoke Valley planters from the time of the Revolution until 1840.[24] Warrenton regularly hosted such events, and Nathaniel Macon's family

21. Harry Roy Merrens, *Colonial North Carolina in the Eighteenth Century: A Study in Historical Geography* (Chapel Hill: University of North Carolina Press, 1964), 156; Charles Christopher Crittenden, *The Commerce of North Carolina, 1763-1789* (New Haven, Conn.: Yale University Press, 1936), 15-17; Risjord, *Chesapeake Politics*, 56, 63; Robinson, *William R. Davie*, 141-147. Eighteenth-century North Carolina was by no means cut off from seaborne commerce. In 1770, over 23,000 tons sailed from the colony's ports—more than New Hampshire, Rhode Island, Connecticut, New Jersey, or Georgia that same year. Furthermore, most North Carolina exports sailed from either Charleston or Norfolk (rather than its own ports), perhaps as much as two-thirds, and are thus not counted in the 1770 total. Not until the much larger tonnages of steam vessels in the nineteenth century would Tar Heel ports seem so deficient. See Carville Earle and Ronald Hoffman, "Urban Development in the Eighteenth-Century South," *Perspectives in American History* 10 (1976): 18n, 27; Kay and Cary, *Slavery in North Carolina*, 28-29.

22. Robinson, *William R. Davie*, 141-142; *North-Carolina Journal* (Halifax), August 29, September 5, October 17, November 14, 1792.

23. Smyth, *Tour in the United States*, 1:61; Robinson, *William R. Davie*, 141-142.

24. Robinson, *William R. Davie*, 145-146; Wilborn, Cathey, and Cross, "The Roanoke Valley," Part I, G; Censer, *North Carolina Planters*, 15. The best account of the horse-racing culture in the Roanoke Valley is

Bible contains in his own hand entries on births, deaths, marriages, and transactions regarding his slaves, his thoroughbreds, and his family members in that order.[25]

The intense rivalries with their Virginia neighbors that characterized gaming in North Carolina border counties like Halifax and Warren carried over into many other activities as well. From at least as early as William Byrd's *History of the Dividing Line* in the 1730s through Joseph Seawell ("Shocco") Jones's defense of Revolutionary zeal in North Carolina in 1834 to arguments about whose troops advanced further at Gettysburg, Cavaliers and Tar Heels have been sniping at one another for centuries over a whole range of claims and counterclaims. Yet the southern counties of Virginia and the northern counties of North Carolina were more alike than different. In early Halifax, Virginia paper money was the principal currency, and Nathaniel Macon always preferred Petersburg as a market for his crops.[26] Business, kinship, cultural, and political ties drove many more Virginia and North Carolina planters together than apart. The long friendships of Macon with Thomas Jefferson and John Randolph of Roanoke testify to such links.

Besides Halifax, the other centripetal force of Nathaniel Macon country was the town of Warrenton, county seat of Warren. With the end of the Tuscarora War, about 1720, white settlers from southern Virginia began crossing the Roanoke to take up lands in what would become Warren County.[27] One such settler was Nathaniel's father, who had established a tobacco plantation on Shocco Creek as detailed earlier. Late in the 1730s, Gideon Macon joined with neighbors Edward Jones and Philemon Hawkins to improve their access to markets. The three planters set out to upgrade the nearby Tuscarora trading path to Petersburg and by 1741 had done so. Their wealth grew accordingly, and by his death in 1762, Gideon had acquired over three thousand acres of land in Warren County, including the parcel near the Roanoke that would become Buck Spring.[28]

Warrenton became the seat of county government in 1779. Its central location and close proximity to part of the Western Great Road made it a logical choice to supersede Bute Courthouse near Macon Manor. In 1786, Warrenton Male

---

Henry W. Lewis, "Horses and Horsemen in Northampton before 1900," *North Carolina Historical Review* 51 (April 1974): 125-148.

25. Macon-Eaton Family Bible, Southern Historical Collection, Wilson Library, University of North Carolina at Chapel Hill. The Macon Papers, State Archives, contain a leather-bound volume entitled *The Racing Calendar Abridged*, published in London in 1829 and inscribed to Macon "from an old and steadfast friend/ J. R. of Roanoke."

26. Risjord, *Chesapeake Politics*, 48-51. When this writer lived in Warrenton as a boy in the 1940s, his Warren County-native parents took him to Virginia Beach (not Nags Head) for summer vacations and to Richmond (not Raleigh) for holiday shopping. Bill Sharpe reported a Halifax resident saying in 1954: "Miller-Rhoads [department store] in Richmond, that's paradise for our women folk." See Sharpe, *New Geography of North Carolina*, 1:157.

27. Wellman, *County of Warren*, 9. Warren County was named in honor of Joseph Warren of Massachusetts, who died at the Battle of Bunker Hill.

28. Wellman, *County of Warren*, 18-24; Dodd, *Life of Nathaniel Macon*, 2-4; Barry, "Nathaniel Macon," 2-3.

COCK-FIGHTING.

In 1786, Halifax County was the most populous in the state, with a population of 10,327 and a black majority. The port town of Halifax, on the Roanoke River, became an important commercial hub for farms in upper North Carolina. Cockfighting was one of the city's popular attractions among wealthy planters. In 1786, Halifax hosted a three-day cockfighting match with rival birds from Virginia, and hundreds of spectators attended the event. This depiction of cockfighting by David Hunter Strother (pen name Porte Crayon) is from *Harper's New Monthly Magazine* 14 (May 1857): 753.

Academy opened to students. By 1794, the town was the crossroads of two important mail routes: Petersburg to Augusta, Georgia, and Halifax to Salisbury.[29] When the prominent merchant and educator Jacob Mordecai settled in Warrenton in 1787, there were a few houses in the village but much potential for growth since tobacco bound for Petersburg and Richmond was being stored there. By the time the Mordecais opened their respected boarding school for girls in 1809, there were several substantial dwellings in town.[30]

The Roanoke Valley passion for horses and fighting birds prevailed in Warrenton as surely as it did in Halifax. The most famous southern horseman of his day, William Ransom Johnson, built a racetrack near Warrenton in the 1790s.

29. Wellman, *County of Warren*, 68-70; Daniel B. Thorp, "Taverns and Tavern Culture on the Southern Colonial Frontier: Rowan County, North Carolina, 1753-1776," *Journal of Southern History* 62 (November 1996): 664-666; Sharpe, *New Geography of North Carolina*, 4:2203.

30. James A. Padgett, ed., "The Life of Alfred Mordecai as Related by Himself," *North Carolina Historical Review* 22 (January 1945): 59, 64-67.

In 1808, his famed thoroughbred, Sir Archie, beat all of the best four-milers from Maryland to Georgia. Nathaniel Macon regularly attended the spring races in Warrenton from as early as 1805.[31] Eleven years later the town had sixteen licensed taverns, reflecting its growth as a social center. By 1824 (and likely earlier), the fall races in Warrenton were regularly accompanied by formal balls and subscription banquets.[32]

From the end of the Revolution until the start of the Civil War, homes of stunning grandeur would be built in Halifax, Warrenton, and their environs. Most of them are gone now, but of the dozen or so that remain a watchful observer can gain a palpable sense of the vitality and immense wealth that characterized the Roanoke Valley elite.[33]

Outside the vibrancy of Halifax and Warrenton and just beyond the rich soil of the Roanoke Valley, most planters in upper North Carolina lived less grand lives. Markets were harder to reach and crops harder to grow. Between 1790 and 1820, North Carolina saw more than 200,000 people emigrate, largely to territories opening up to the south and west.[34] Nathaniel Macon observed both the plenty of some of his neighbors and the precarious marginality of others. Although he was a successful planter, Macon was never as rich as Roanoke families like the Eatons and Williamses. He worked hard at Buck Spring when there and when away kept as close an eye on it as mail communications of the day permitted. Macon knew about the perilous balance of certain farming operations from close personal experience.

At the time of the American Revolution, over 95 percent of Americans farmed.[35] In North Carolina agriculture was not just an economic force but a way of life. At Macon's Buck Spring (and to the Piedmont south and west), tobacco was the principal crop, even after cotton production accelerated after 1800. Roanoke Valley planters grew corn for their own use but also for sale (unlike most Tar Heel farmers), and other crops included wheat and a variety of fruits and vegetables. Livestock and poultry were everywhere, and hogs often ran wild

---

31. Wilborn, Cathey, and Cross, "The Roanoke Valley," Part I, G; Wellman, *County of Warren*, 77-81. Two days of spring races in Warrenton were advertised in the *Raleigh Register*, May 27, 1800.

32. Wellman, *County of Warren*, 94; *Warrenton Reporter*, October 22, 1824. The Warrenton fall races began on September 30, 1829, and lasted four days with balls on the evenings of the second and third days. See advertisement in *Halifax Minerva*, September 3, 1829.

33. Catherine W. Bishir, *North Carolina Architecture* (Chapel Hill: University of North Carolina Press, 1990), 88-96, 253-257. Most of the grander dwellings in the region were built after Macon died, but he certainly knew some splendid early examples that no longer exist, like Willie Jones's "Grove," just outside Halifax. At the 1835 Constitutional Convention, Macon said that he would rather live in North Carolina than anywhere else. There were not "so many splendid houses, but the people generally had comfortable dwellings and good plantations." See *Proceedings and Debates of the Convention, 1835*, 91-92.

34. C. Cathey, *Agricultural Developments in North Carolina*, 25-26, 45-47.

35. Bill McKibben, "Some Versions of Pastoral," *New York Review of Books*, July 11, 1996. By 1996, fewer than 1 percent of Americans farmed full time.

Wealthy northeastern North Carolina planters were passionate about horse racing. William Ransom Johnson, the premier southern horseman of his day, built a racetrack near Warrenton in the 1790s. In 1808, his famed thoroughbred, Sir Archie, beat all of the best four-milers from Maryland to Georgia. Nathaniel Macon often attended the spring races in Warrenton. By 1824, the fall races were regularly accompanied by formal balls and subscription banquets. Engraving of Sir Archie from Henry William Herbert, *Frank Forester's Horse and Horsemanship*, 2 vols. (New York: Stringer and Townsend, 1857), 1: facing 122.

foraging for food while awaiting slaughter. North Carolina farms were generally smaller and more self-sufficient than those in other southern states. In fact, the average agricultural producing unit in North Carolina actually shrank in acreage between 1800 and 1860 as the white population increased. Most farmers (and planters too) followed the same practices year after year, usually to the detriment of overall production.[36] If thousands of Tar Heel farmers emigrated in search of a better living, the vast majority stayed rooted to places they knew, survived on, and even occasionally prospered from. Many would subscribe to the warm sentiments expressed by Macon to a fellow planter in 1828: "Fine weather for planting corn or any other kind of plantation work, to those who have it [to] do. . . . with you the birds are singing, all your domestic fowls lively, gay, strutting and making a cheerful noise, your people employed, at work . . . all merry & in good humor, this is truly faring well. . . ."[37]

36. C. Cathey, *Agricultural Developments in North Carolina*, 49, 107, 118-120, 126, 181, 194-196. In 1823, Macon said of Buck Spring: "on one plantation the war [of 1812] system has been continued, that is not much for sale & buy less, it is true the land is poor and stony, but it is honestly made, enough to have full bellies and warm clothes for any time of the year." Nathaniel Macon to Bolling Hall, June 20, 1823, Hall Papers.

37. Nathaniel Macon to Weldon Edwards, March 28, 1828, Macon Papers.

When he became twenty-one in late 1779, Macon took up residence at Buck Spring. The five hundred acres (and three slaves) devised to him were in the northeastern corner of Warren County. Macon would acquire more land over time, and at his death in 1837, Buck Spring plantation consisted of 1,945 acres and nearly eighty slaves.[38] His dwelling was a modest but efficient structure of logs covered with weatherboard outside and an oak ceiling inside. The house measured sixteen feet by twenty, and it sat in a grove of white oaks seventy-five yards from a spring where deer watered, hence the name Buck Spring. The structure was originally intended as a weaving room in a larger complex of plantation buildings and had one large room with a fireplace downstairs and a loft above. Beneath the dwelling was a wine cellar.[39]

When Macon married Hannah Plummer of Warren County in 1783 and brought her to Buck Spring, there was a kitchen within fifteen yards of the dwelling. It was eighteen by twenty feet and almost identical to the residence except for a bigger fireplace. The downstairs was the dining room, and the two Macon daughters, Betsy and Seigniora (born in 1784 and 1787), slept upstairs. As they grew older, they would entertain friends at Buck Spring, and quilts would be spread on the floors of the kitchen to accommodate girls visiting overnight.[40] Macon intended to build a larger house for his family and had selected a site about a hundred yards from the small dwelling, but with the death of Hannah early in 1790, he abandoned such plans. The modest residence that was home for the rest of his life and in which he would die in 1837 was as unpretentious and solid as its owner.[41]

Over time, Macon would add a dairy, a smokehouse, and a granary to the site, all in the same basic style as the dwelling. A barn, stables, and slave cabins located a couple of hundred yards from the residence lined a road that ran through the middle of the plantation. A bedroom in the dairy loft was furnished for visitors and

38. Bonath, "Buck Spring Archaeology," 1-2; B. Cathey, "Nathaniel Macon and Buck Spring," Nathaniel Macon Section; Cotten, *Life of Hon. Nathaniel Macon*, 249. Shortly after the marriage of his younger daughter in 1807, Macon divided his real holdings into three parts, giving one each to his two married daughters and retaining one. He loaned eleven slaves apiece to each daughter and then bequeathed those slaves to his daughters' heirs in his 1837 will. See Macon's will in Warren County Original Wills, 1779-1936, State Archives.

39. Mrs. V. L. Pendleton, "The Home of Nat. [sic] Macon," *The North Carolina Teacher* 6 (December 1888): 198-202; Bonath, "Buck Spring Archaeology," 3-5; B. Cathey, "Nathaniel Macon and Buck Spring," Nathaniel Macon and Buck Spring Section. A reconstruction of the residence and a large restored corncrib stand on their original sites and may be visited by the public. Warren County owns the sites and several acres surrounding them.

40. Bonath, "Buck Spring Archaeology," 6; B. Cathey, "Nathaniel Macon and Buck Spring," Nathaniel Macon and Buck Spring Section; Cotten, *Life of Hon. Nathaniel Macon*, 80, 248. Edward Cotten, a contemporary visitor to Buck Spring, notes that Macon especially enjoyed the company of young people.

41. B. Cathey, "Nathaniel Macon and Buck Spring," Nathaniel Macon Section. Macon's six-year-old son, Plummer, died in 1792. Macon did not stand for election to Congress (despite earlier pleas from constituents) until after Hannah's death. Although his daughters grew to adulthood, they both died years before their father.

was the favored spot of John Randolph of Roanoke on his not-infrequent visits to Buck Spring.[42] Close political allies in Congress from Randolph's entry there in 1799, Macon and Randolph were even closer personal friends. As profound as was their devotion to Old Republican principles, matching it was their passion for their region, for deer and fox hunting, for the dogs of the chase, and for thoroughbred horses.[43]

To own large plantation houses would have seemed ostentatious of the widowed Macon and the unmarried Randolph. It was Thomas Jefferson who had called Macon "Ultimus Romanorum"—the last of the Romans, and the characterization was apt. In *De Officiis*, Cicero had said that the dwelling of a magnanimous man should not be large but just sufficient to accommodate the needs of family and friends. Macon and Randolph, who read and admired Cicero, surely agreed.[44]

Macon worked in the fields of Buck Spring alongside his slaves until age precluded that in 1817. Congress was adjourned during most of planting and harvesting time, and Macon hired an overseer those months when he was away in Washington.[45] His correspondence through the years often reflects his interest in, concern for, and pleasure in plantation work and play. Writing from Buck Spring in September 1802, Macon reported a good corn crop, better cotton, but poor tobacco. Over the years until his death, Macon would report on the ups and downs of various crops, including wheat and sundry fruits and vegetables, but corn, cotton,

42. Bonath, "Buck Spring Archaeology," 19-22. Drawings in this report convey a sense of the layout of the plantation. Randolph's own plantation, "Roanoke," was about sixty miles from Buck Spring in Virginia and shared many similarities in building design and physical layout. See William Cabell Bruce, *John Randolph of Roanoke, 1773-1833*, 2 vols. (New York: G. P. Putnam's Sons, 1922), 2:355-357; Dawidoff, *Education of John Randolph*, 36.

43. B. Cathey, "Nathaniel Macon and Buck Spring," Nathaniel Macon and Buck Spring Section; Cotten, *Life of Hon. Nathaniel Macon*, 129. Over fifty pedigreed horses were foaled at Buck Spring during Macon's lifetime.

44. John Hill Wheeler, *Historical Sketches of North Carolina from 1524 to 1851*, 2 vols. (Philadelphia: Lippincott, Grambo and Co., 1851), 2:436; Barry, "Nathaniel Macon," 1, 239; Eugene D. Genovese, *The Southern Tradition: The Achievement and Limitations of an American Conservatism* (Cambridge, Mass.: Harvard University Press, 1994), 4, 68. Edward Livingston of New York and later Louisiana called Macon "the Cato of Republicanism," and Thomas Hart Benton said that Macon "was the real Cincinnatus of America."

45. Thomas Hart Benton, *Thirty Years' View . . . from 1820 to 1850* (1875; reprint, New York: George Braziller, 1963), 33; Cotten, *Life of Hon. Nathaniel Macon*, 227, 252-253. Macon usually employed men from the neighboring Shearin family as overseers. Cotten recounts that when Macon's son-in-law William Eaton once visited Buck Spring to check on its condition, he pointed out to Lewis Shearin that some sheep in an enclosed pasture looked sickly and ought to be let out to graze. Shearin replied that before leaving for Washington Mr. Macon had told him that the sheep were to be kept penned, and so they would remain even if it meant the death of the whole flock. Eaton told this story to the congressman upon his return, and Macon was delighted.

When Macon turned twenty-one in 1779, he took up residence in one of the richest agricultural areas in North Carolina, in the northeastern corner of Warren County. His five-hundred-acre plantation, Buck Spring, was four miles from the Roanoke River and close to the social and commercial centers of Warrenton and Halifax. Macon's home was a modest one-room log structure covered with weatherboard. Originally intended as a weaving room, the dwelling had a fireplace downstairs, a loft, and a wine cellar. Photograph of Macon's home at Buck Spring courtesy of the State Archives.

Macon took a great deal of interest in both the chores and pleasures of plantation life. He worked in the fields alongside his slaves until 1817 and apparently was a stern but not vicious master. He deemed slavery a curse but could see "no means of getting rid of it." His plantation primarily produced corn, cotton, and tobacco, but Macon also grew other crops, including wheat and various fruits and vegetables. This photograph of the corncrib at Buck Spring is by Michael Southern, courtesy of the State Archives.

and tobacco dominated his subsequent recountings.[46] He took palpable pleasure in reporting on fox and deer hunts and the dogs and horses so essential to the sport. At Buck Spring, Macon kept as many as ten thoroughbred horses for guests to use during hunts.[47] Even when away in Congress, both Macon and John Randolph

46. Kemp P. Battle, ed., *Letters of Nathaniel Macon, John Steele, and William Barry Grove* (Chapel Hill: University of North Carolina, 1902), 22-23; Nathaniel Macon to Albert Gallatin, June 28, 1806, June 30, 1807, Albert Gallatin Papers, New-York Historical Society, New York City (photocopies in State Archives, Raleigh), hereinafter cited as Gallatin Papers; Nathaniel Macon to William H. Crawford, October 13, 1817, William H. Crawford Papers, Duke Special Collections; Elizabeth Gregory McPherson, ed., "Letters from Nathaniel Macon to John Randolph of Roanoke," *North Carolina Historical Review* 39 (April 1962): 200-201, 209-211; Nathaniel Macon to Weldon Edwards, December 20, 1829, November 8, 1834, January 20, 1835, Katherine Clark Pendleton Conway Collection, Private Collections, State Archives, hereinafter cited as Conway Collection; Nathaniel Macon to Weldon Edwards, August 10, 1833, May 20, 1834, Weldon N. Edwards Papers, Southern Historical Collection, hereinafter cited as Edwards Papers.

47. Edwin Mood Wilson, *The Congressional Career of Nathaniel Macon Followed by Letters from Mr. Macon and Willie P. Mangum with Notes by Kemp P. Battle* (Chapel Hill: University of North Carolina, 1900), 73-74; McPherson, "Letters from Nathaniel Macon to John Randolph," 201-202; Nathaniel Macon to Weldon Edwards, August 10, 1833, Edwards Papers; Barry, "Nathaniel Macon," 271; Dodd, *Life of Nathaniel Macon*, 371. Roanoke Valley hunts for fox and deer were done on horseback with packs of dogs pursuing the prey. Hunters carried guns and wore everyday clothes, not fashionable sporting outfits. An excellent description of a deer hunt in eastern North Carolina in 1777 appears in E. Watson, *Men and Times of the Revolution*, 38-39. That method of hunting continued in Warren County through the nineteenth century into the twentieth. See Reynolds Price, *Clear Pictures: First Loves, First Guides* (New York: Atheneum, 1989), 135-138.

had thoroughbreds and dogs with them for frequent riding and occasional hunting near Georgetown.[48]

The labor force at Buck Spring consisted of African American slaves. Basing their judgments in the paternalistic ideal of the day, his contemporaries cited Macon as a good master. Friend and biographer Edward Cotten wrote in 1840, "Never had slaves a kinder master." Macon personally attended to providing basic food, clothing, shelter, and moral instruction.[49] During the Missouri Compromise debates in January 1820, Macon had said on the floor of Congress in response to criticisms of slavery by another member, "I sincerely wish that he . . . would go home with me, or some other Southern member, and witness the meeting between the slaves and the owner, and see the glad faces and the hearty shaking of hands. . . ."[50] But to fit Macon into the paternalistic mold is not to say that he viewed his slaves as "children." He made it clear more than once that his slaves were property to be used and disposed of as his needs dictated.[51]

As an on-site master, Macon was stern but not vicious. He fretted over sick slaves and sometimes personally attended the ill. When one of his bondsmen ran away from Buck Spring in 1835, Macon was pleased when he returned "without quarrel" three days later.[52] In the complex relationship of master and slave that was a centerpiece of the plantation world, Macon and Randolph, accompanied by trusted slaves, more than once headed into the woods for overnight forays of shooting, followed by cleaning and dressing game with knives. Macon's fondness for Randolph's body servants (and hunting veterans) was expressed in a letter written to the Virginian while he was minister to Russia in 1830: "Tell Old man Essex, Johnny & Juba Howdye & that I have a regard for their fidelity & attachment to you."[53]

While Macon (along with most of his white contemporaries) viewed African Americans as inferior, he fully recognized their potential to fight for freedom.

48. Dodd, *Life of Nathaniel Macon*, 174, 302; Bruce, *John Randolph of Roanoke*, 1:560. Macon, Randolph, and other Old Republicans usually boarded at the same house in Washington during congressional sessions. There were stables nearby.

49. Cotten, *Life of Hon. Nathaniel Macon*, 77; Weldon N. Edwards, *Memoir of Nathaniel Macon of North Carolina* (Raleigh, N.C.: Raleigh Register Steam Power Press, 1862), 14, 18. Macon required his slaves to gather at his house on Sundays when he read the Bible to them. See Dodd, *Life of Nathaniel Macon*, 376.

50. Quoted in Calhoon, "Agrarian and Evangelical Culture," 185. No less an authority than Norman Risjord calls this the first defense of slavery as a "positive good" ever made in Congress. See Norman K. Risjord, *The Old Republicans: Southern Conservatism in the Age of Jefferson* (New York: Columbia University Press, 1965), 215.

51. Nathaniel Macon to Weldon Edwards, May 12, 1828, Macon Papers; Nathaniel Macon speech notes (undated but likely 1828), Conway Collection; *Proceedings and Debates of the Convention, 1835*, 69-70.

52. Dawidoff, *Education of John Randolph*, 52; McPherson, "Letters from Nathaniel Macon to John Randolph," 205-207; Nathaniel Macon to Weldon Edwards, January 20, 1835, Conway Collection; Nathaniel Macon to Weldon Edwards, May 20, 1834, Edwards Papers.

53. Dodd, *Life of Nathaniel Macon*, 150-151; Bruce, *John Randolph of Roanoke*, 2:592-594; McPherson, "Letters from Nathaniel Macon to John Randolph," 209-211.

He acknowledged that many slaves and some free blacks had fought for the patriot cause in the American Revolution, but "they were made no part of the political family" in doing so, nor should they have been in his view. He also knew of the Gabriel Prosser plot in Richmond in 1800 and a slave uprising in Bertie County in 1802.[54] African Americans could and did rebel, and Macon knew it.

In 1797, Congressman Macon had called slavery a curse but could see "no means of getting rid of it." As early as 1818, he had deplored the prevailing loose interpretation of the U.S. Constitution (in order to establish banks and fund internal improvements like roads and canals), because if Congress could do such things without explicit authority, it could also emancipate every slave. That course, Macon said, meant chaos.[55] As he told John C. Calhoun in 1823, "to free [slaves] in the south would be the means of destroying either the blacks or whites as at San Domingo [in 1791]."[56]

Perhaps nothing speaks more clearly of Macon and his "people" than the disposition of his slaves in his will probated in the summer of 1837. He gave to each of "the negroes who work in or out a store shirt or shift." He divided his slaves among his grandchildren with a request (but not a requirement) "to keep families as much together as may be practicable or convenient." In the case of four slaves (of the seventy-seven he owned), Macon made special provision: "my faithfull Servant Phil and his wife China" plus their present and future increase went to grandson Nathaniel Macon Martin. Husband and wife Ephraim and Lucy could choose which of the grandchildren they would belong to; if they chose none of them, they would then go to Francis Thornton, Macon's kinsman and neighbor.[57]

Thus, for years of unpaid labor, Macon's "people" received an article of clothing and transfer to various new owners—even in the case of the two couples specially provided for. The rationale for such a system was defined with stark precision by Justice Thomas Ruffin in the North Carolina case of *State v. Mann* (1829). A noted

54. *Proceedings and Debates of the Convention, 1835,* 69-70; *Raleigh Register,* October 7, 1800; Nathaniel Macon to Albert Gallatin, June 20, 1802, Gallatin Papers. Macon's racial views closely resembled those of Thomas Jefferson. See Paul Finkelman, "Jefferson and Slavery: 'Treason against the Hopes of the World,' " in *Jeffersonian Legacies,* ed. Peter S. Onuf (Charlottesville: University Press of Virginia, 1993), 184-186. In Bertie County in 1802, patrollers discovered in Colerain a note containing the names of the alleged rebels. The suspects were tried, and altogether, eleven were executed, six deported, and twenty more whipped and brutalized. Alan D. Watson, *Bertie County: A Brief History* (Raleigh: Division of Archives and History, Department of Cultural Resources, 1982), 11.

55. William K. Boyd, "Nathaniel Macon in National Legislation," *Trinity College Historical Society Papers* (Series 4, 1900), 77-78; Wilson, *Congressional Career of Macon Followed by Letters,* 46-50. To begin to comprehend the role of slavery in the history of North Carolina, the best starting point is Jeffrey J. Crow, Paul D. Escott, and Flora J. Hatley, *A History of African Americans in North Carolina* (Raleigh: Division of Archives and History, Department of Cultural Resources, 1992), chaps. 1-4.

56. Wilson, *Congressional Career of Macon Followed by Letters,* 67-74.

57. Warren County Original Wills, 1779-1936, State Archives; Slave inventory (undated but in hand of Weldon Edwards, executor), Conway Collection. The real property at Buck Spring was divided between Macon's eldest grandsons, William Eaton Jr. and Nathaniel Macon Martin.

Virginia and North Carolina planters were closely connected by business, kinship, and cultural and political ties. Macon, in fact, preferred Petersburg as a market for his crops. The Antifederalist Virginia congressman John Randolph of Roanoke was one of Macon's close political allies as well as a close personal friend. Randolph frequently visited Buck Spring, and both enjoyed riding and hunting with their dogs and thoroughbred horses. This portrait of John Randolph by Gilbert Stuart is courtesy of the National Gallery of Art, Washington, D.C.

jurist on the highest court, Ruffin wrote: "The end [of slavery] is the profit of the master, his security and the public safety. . . . The power of the master must be absolute, to render the submission of the slave perfect."[58] Macon, the planter, embraced the reasoning undergirding Ruffin's argument.

Other bequests in Macon's will illustrate his life-style at Buck Spring, his close friendship with John Randolph of Roanoke, his reading interests, and hi love of sport. Carpentry and blacksmithing tools went to grandsons as did turkeys, geese,

58. *State v. Mann*, 1829, in Willie Lee Rose, ed., *A Documentary History of Slavery in North America* (New York: Oxford University Press, 1976), 219-224; Censer, *North Carolina Planters*, 144-145.

hogs, and "fruit of every kind." They also divided the silver flatware given to Macon by Randolph. Granddaughters got punch bowls, ladles, flatware, wash basins, and bed linens. The large quantities of flatware and serving pieces testified to Macon's practice of entertaining guests. One grandson received gold sleeve buttons that John Randolph had given his old friend; another, a bag of English shillings from the famous Virginian. To Sen. Thomas Hart Benton went Randolph's pocketknife.[59]

Macon's books (including the family Bible and Sir William Blackstone's *Commentaries on the Laws of England*) plus pamphlets and public documents went almost entirely to his eldest grandson. Exceptions included his "encyclopedia" to another grandson, two volumes "of [James] Anderson on agriculture" to his kinsman and biographer, Congressman Weldon N. Edwards, and individual volumes that he designated with labels to specific people.[60]

Items associated with hunting went to family and friends, including a long gun, a short gun, a shot bag, a powder horn, a spyglass, and some blowing horns (to rally the dogs). His hounds went to a neighbor. Some live deer and a fawn were bequeathed to neighbors and a grandson. His chickens were to be divided among family and "cockfighting friends." His son-in-law William Eaton got "Hard Rain," a thoroughbred.[61]

Finally, Macon instructed his executor: "you may give the people, who may come, to the funeral preached over me, a dinner & grog as you may please or not give as you may please." It pleased Weldon Edwards to do so. In July 1837, the *Raleigh Register* reported that between one thousand and fifteen hundred whites and several hundred blacks attended Macon's funeral and that no one left hungry or thirsty. A Baptist minister preached the service.[62]

---

59. Warren County Original Wills, 1779-1936, State Archives; Estate inventory (undated, Weldon Edwards's hand), Conway Collection. Randolph had died in 1833. It was Benton who would publish the story of Macon once drawing a knife in defense of Randolph during an altercation with some military officers in a Philadelphia theater. See Benton, *Thirty Years' View*, 33.

60. Benton, *Thirty Years' View*, 33; Edwards, *Memoir of Nathaniel Macon*, 6. The North Carolina Museum of History has four of Macon's books, including works by Capt. John Smith, by Adam Smith, and *The Book of Common Prayer*. These accessions are noted in an appendix in B. Cathey, "Nathaniel Macon and Buck Spring." This writer owns a volume of eighteenth-century satirical verse that contains this bookplate: "Nathanael [sic] Macon/ of Warren County/ North-Carolina." As previously noted, the family Bible is at the Southern Historical Collection. It is the Clarendon Press (of Oxford University) printing of 1795.

61. Benton, *Thirty Years' View*, 33; Edwards, *Memoir of Nathaniel Macon*, 6. As a boy, this writer knew Nathaniel Macon Thornton, a descendant of Macon. He would tell a family story attributed to Macon. The master of Buck Spring directed that when he was buried, those present should drag a fox tail around his grave with hounds in pursuit while pouring whiskey on the ground covering him. If that did not rouse him, then he was truly dead. Macon kept a wine cellar underneath his home for guests but drank corn whiskey himself. Dodd, *Life of Nathaniel Macon*, 372; Bonath, "Buck Spring Archaeology," 16.

62. Warren County Original Wills, State Archives; B. Cathey, "Nathaniel Macon and Buck Spring," appendix Cotten, *Life of Hon. Nathaniel Macon*, 262-266.

No one who reads Macon's correspondence can doubt his admiration for the Bible. More than once, he bemoaned Americans' pursuit of "false gods" (like financial credit and political patronage) as the children of Israel had done thousands of years earlier. Such error meant destruction; was that not the clear lesson of the Book of Judges?[63] While Macon read the Bible to his slaves on Sunday and often attended services at a Baptist meeting near Buck Spring, he never joined a church. The Macon family had been Huguenots in France before migrating to Virginia in the seventeenth century, and then Episcopalians. Young Nathaniel attended the Presbyterian College of New Jersey, and his wife belonged to that denomination. But like his good friend John Randolph, Macon declined church membership.[64]

Macon stated his religious views most clearly late in life at the 1835 Constitutional Convention. During debates over the "Protestant test" qualification in the original State Constitution of 1776, he stepped down from his chair as president to argue from the floor. Macon said that that clause (which required officeholders to be Protestants) was the only part of the venerable constitution that he had ever voiced objection to outside of North Carolina. Man alone, he declared, is responsible to God for his religious faith: "If a Hindoo were to come among us, and was fully qualified to discharge the duties of any office to which he might aspire, his religion would not constitute an objection. . . . He [Macon] had always thought that a mixture of Politics and Religion was the very essence of hypocrisy." He pointed out that North Carolina had been discovered by Catholics and that the Glorious Revolution of 1688 in England had not "done any essential good—for, sir, from that has sprung the bigoted intolerance, which I am sorry to say has descended to this generation, and is too plainly manifested here [in this debate]." Macon said that fears that Roman Catholics would overrun the country were as probable "as that a mouse would kill a buffaloe."[65]

As to his own public practice of religion, Macon said that he was inclined toward the Baptists but "was far from believing in all their doctrines." In the final analysis, church affiliation counted for little in Macon's view: "If he faithfully discharged all his duties on earth, and obeyed the precepts of the Gospel, he would not be asked, when he reached Heaven, to what sect he belonged." Although the convention did away with the Protestant test, it did propose in the new constitution a profession of Christianity for officeholding. Macon preferred no

---

63. Nathaniel Macon to Albert Gallatin, February 14, 1824, Gallatin Papers; Wilson, *Congressional Career of Macon Followed by Letters*, 84-86. In the 1826 letter to Bartlett Yancey printed in Wilson's book, Macon writes that "the whole Bible contains great knowledge of the principles of government."

64. Dodd, *Life of Nathaniel Macon*, 2-4, 376-380; Barry, "Nathaniel Macon," 14, 26; Boyd, "Nathaniel Macon in National Legislation," 74. Barry reports that Macon did experience a religious conversion as a young man.

65. *Proceedings and Debates of the Convention, 1835*, 226, 246-248.

Willie Jones's Federalist nephew-in-law, William R. Davie, was also a member of the northeastern North Carolina planter elite. Davie, a Halifax lawyer and Revolutionary War officer, was chiefly responsible for the bill chartering the University of North Carolina. Like most of that generation of Revolutionary leaders in the South, Davie and Jones, as well as Macon, consistently advocated the value of education. This photograph of the William R. Davie home, "Loretta," is courtesy of the State Archives.

test at all but voted for the new language as an improvement over the 1776 constitution.[66]

Macon had undertaken service in the 1835 convention reluctantly. It would be his penultimate public act. The following year he agreed to stand as a presidential elector for his political ally and close personal friend Martin Van Buren of New York, who had once said that he valued Macon's opinion above all others. Having voted for Van Buren, Macon spent his remaining months at Buck Spring removed from the concerns of the larger world, except for occasionally visiting friends or corresponding with Democrats seeking his counsel. He no longer even subscribed to a newspaper.[67]

When Macon had retired from the U.S. Senate in 1828, he was almost seventy years old. Several factors weighed in his decision: his increasing loss of hearing and eyesight; the deaths of his only surviving children (Seigniora in 1825 and Betsy in 1827); the death of Betsy's husband, William Martin, a Granville County planter, in 1828, thus leaving their eleven children orphans; and Macon's recognition that the Psalmist allots a man seventy years and no more. In a letter written at Buck Spring in the fall of 1828, Macon informed the North Carolina legislature that "age and infirmity" made it necessary for him to resign his offices as U.S. senator, trustee of the University of North Carolina, and justice of the peace of Warren County. He concluded "that no person can be under more obligation to a State, than I am to North Carolina, nor feel more strongly & that duty alone has induced me to resign."[68]

Even before resigning from the Senate, Macon knew that the country he had lived in since colonial times was changing at the national, state, and local levels. Nothing so manifestly demonstrated that change as did the swelling interest in internal improvements—road construction, canal building, swamp drainage, railroad construction, and similar transportation and technological developments.

---

66. *Proceedings and Debates of the Convention, 1835*, 246-248, 331-332; Harold J. Counihan, "The North Carolina Constitutional Convention of 1835: A Study in Jacksonian Democracy," *North Carolina Historical Review* 46 (October 1969): 351-353.

67. Nathaniel Macon to Weldon Edwards, May 24, 1835, Conway Collection; *Proceedings and Debates of the Convention, 1835*, 8-9; John C. Fitzpatrick, ed., *Autobiography of Martin Van Buren* (Washington: Government Printing Office, 1920), 221; Martin Van Buren to Henry Fitts, March 25, 1839, Martin Van Buren Papers, Library of Congress, Washington (typed transcripts in Private Collections, State Archives); Cotten, *Life of Hon. Nathaniel Macon*, 263-266; Barry, "Nathaniel Macon," 272, 293. Macon thanked Van Buren for a picture of the vice-president sent early in 1836 but reiterated his dislike for such things. Macon gave it to his first great-grandson, Van Buren Martin. See Nathaniel Macon to Martin Van Buren, January 24, 1836, Macon Papers.

68. Nathaniel Macon to William Eaton Jr., April 13, 1826, Macon Papers; Benton, *Thirty Years' View*, 29; Nathaniel Macon to Weldon Edwards, May 20, 1834, Edwards Papers; Barry, "Nathaniel Macon," 261-263, 272-273; Resignation of Nathaniel Macon, November 14, 1828, Session of 1828-1829, General Assembly Session Records, State Archives. Seigniora Macon had married the very wealthy Warren County planter William Eaton. The spelling of "Seigniora" is that used by her father in recording her birth and death in the family Bible. Dodd and some others use a different spelling.

In 1836, Macon agreed to stand as a presidential elector for his political ally and close personal friend Democrat Martin Van Buren of New York, who affirmed that he valued Macon's opinion above all others. Macon apparently supported the emergent Democratic Party's coalition of southern planters and northern Republicans. Engraving of Van Buren from Johnson, Fry, and Co. Publishers, New York, courtesy of the author.

The role of federal support for such improvements would be a major battleground in Congress from the early days of the new nation. Macon, like Randolph and other Old Republicans, regularly opposed the "loose construction" of the U.S. Constitution necessary to permit federal funds for internal improvements.[69]

While Macon resisted federal funding of internal improvements, the matter of state support was a different proposition. Better still were various private undertakings to effect infrastructure changes. Agriculture pursued on independent farms was Macon's economic ideal, but he also recognized the inevitable lure of improved market access.[70]

Between 1784 and 1825, the North Carolina General Assembly incorporated thirty-three private navigation companies. In 1790, the legislature chartered the Dismal Swamp Canal Company to connect the Pasquotank River with the Elizabeth River in Virginia. It was in service for small craft by 1808. The Roanoke Navigation Company was chartered in 1812 and organized in 1816. As it would in several other projects, the state purchased stock in the company over the years, especially after prodding by Archibald Murphey in 1815. Macon himself owned stock in the company. Between 1823 and 1834, locks were being constructed around the town of Weldon near Halifax. Steamboats were regularly on the Roanoke by 1821, and the Roanoke Navigation Company was the most successful such endeavor in antebellum North Carolina.[71] When the Dismal Swamp Canal was improved to accommodate steamboats in 1829, traffic in Halifax and Weldon swelled in response. Local newspapers routinely reported on the growing volume of goods and passengers moving up and down the Roanoke River.[72] As startling as were the improvements to waterways, they would soon be surpassed by the coming of the railroads. The first serious proposal for rail development in North Carolina came during 1827-1828 from Joseph Caldwell, president of the University of North Carolina, in a series of articles in the *Raleigh Register*. During the 1830s, the Raleigh and Gaston (a town on the Roanoke in Northampton County) and the

69. Russell Kirk, *Randolph of Roanoke: A Study in Conservative Thought* (Chicago: University of Chicago Press, 1951), 60, 68; John Lauritz Larson, "Jefferson's Union and the Problem of Internal Improvements," in Onuf, *Jeffersonian Legacies*, 359, 363; Risjord, *Old Republicans*, 171; Zane L. Miller, "Senator Nathaniel Macon and the Public Domain, 1815-1828," *North Carolina Historical Review* 38 (October 1961): 484, 491-492.

70. Harry L. Watson, "Squire Oldway and His Friends: Opposition to Internal Improvements in Antebellum North Carolina," *North Carolina Historical Review* 54 (April 1977): 107-109, 110.

71. Charles Clinton Weaver, *Internal Improvements in North Carolina Previous to 1860* (Baltimore: Johns Hopkins Press, 1903), 57-62, 69-72; Alan D. Watson, "North Carolina and Internal Improvements, 1783-1861: The Case of Inland Navigation," *North Carolina Historical Review* 74 (January 1997), 39-41, 51, 71; Wilson, *Congressional Career of Macon Followed by Letters*, 73-74.

72. *Halifax Minerva*, June 25, July 9, August 27, 1829; *Roanoke Advocate* (Halifax), March 13, May 13, 1830. Macon observed the increased traffic around Halifax and Weldon but continued to use Petersburg as his market out of "ancient attachment" and because one of his grandsons lived there. See McPherson, "Letters from Nathaniel Macon to John Randolph," 207-211.

Wilmington and Weldon Railroads were chartered, and both were completed in 1840. An earlier rail line from Petersburg to Weldon had opened in 1833. In 1836, the Raleigh and Gaston right-of-way was laid out in Warren County, and wooden ties were being put down the following year.[73] When completed in 1840, the line passed within five miles of Buck Spring. Macon disliked change while recognizing its positive attraction for so many.[74] The same man who used Petersburg as a market year after year when closer markets opened in his own state, who was fascinated by but refused to adopt new cultivation techniques, who was delighted by an overseer who would have willingly let sheep die rather than disobey their owner's instructions, who dressed plainly in the fashion of the 1780s throughout his adult life, and who hoped that the South would cling to its agrarian past and remain uncorrupted by the commercialism on the rise in other sections, did not readily embrace new ways.[75]

During his last months at Buck Spring, Macon rarely ventured away from it. His friend and protégé, Weldon Edwards, would sometimes ride over from his plantation, Poplar Mount, about fifteen miles away, and the rare day-visitor or relative dropping by did not linger. The happy days of the hunt were over for the old man. On June 18, 1837, he wrote a letter to the new president of the United States, his friend Martin Van Buren, introducing Macon's kinsman Joseph Seawell Jones, who was hand delivering it. "My life is fast giving away," Macon wrote, "and I know I must soon die."[76]

Macon knew himself well. Although he experienced chest and stomach spasms early in June, he continued to ride his horse over the plantation grounds daily. About June 22, the discomfort increased, and he was partially confined to his house. Friends and neighbors began to drop by each day to check on him. On the morning of June 29, Macon arose early as was his usual practice. He shaved, dressed and conversed with those present. About 10:00 A.M. while sitting in a

73. Allen W. Trelease, *The North Carolina Railroad, 1849-1871, and the Modernization of North Carolina* (Chapel Hill: University of North Carolina Press, 1991), 12-13; Wilborn, Cathey, and Cross, "Roanoke Valley," Part I, H; Wellman, *County of Warren*, 112-114.

74. Macon once told Thomas Jefferson that "improvements in the United States have brought machines to do almost everything but speak." See Elizabeth G. McPherson, ed., "Unpublished Letters from North Carolinians to Jefferson," parts 1 and 2, *North Carolina Historical Review* 12 (July/October 1935): 374.

75. Nathaniel Macon to Bolling Hall, June 20, 1823, February 10, 1824, Hall Papers; H. Watson, "Squire Oldway and His Friends," 116-119. In a fascinating letter to Bartlett Yancey in 1828, Macon defined the South physically, not politically (e.g., the Mason-Dixon line). The northern boundary of the South was the south bank of the James River in Virginia: "No long leaf pine North of the James River nor live oak north of new point comfort, the long leaf pine and live oak, are the boundaries of the South." See Wilson, *Congressional Career of Macon Followed by Letters*, 100-103.

76. Nathaniel Macon to Weldon Edwards, July 17, 1836, Conway Collection; Elizabeth G. McPherson, ed., "Unpublished Letters from North Carolinians to Van Buren," *North Carolina Historical Review* 15 (January 1938): 71. Appendix B of Barry, "Nathaniel Macon," contains a checklist of Macon's outgoing correspondence. It confirms that this letter to Van Buren was the last in Macon's hand.

Like Randolph and other Old Republicans, Macon regularly opposed federal funding for internal improvements. However, he supported state and private efforts at road construction, canal building, swamp drainage, and railroad construction. He owned stock in the Roanoke Navigation Company, one of thirty-three private navigation companies chartered by the state between 1784 and 1825, and saw the volume of goods and people transported on the river and its canals grow steadily during that period. Photograph of the Roanoke River canal aqueduct by William S. Price Jr., reproduced with permission.

chair, he complained of more spasms and was helped into bed. There he died "without a struggle" (Edward Cotten reported) and "sunk to rest without pain or suffering" (as Weldon Edwards related).[77]

His plain coffin was buried at a site about three hundred yards east of his home. Weldon Edwards reported that Macon told him the site was "so barren no one will ever desire to cultivate it." He further directed that stones thrown up by plows working the land be used to cover him.[78] Good farmland should not be devoted to the dead.

77. Cotten, *Life of Hon. Nathaniel Macon*, 263-266; Edwards, *Memoir of Nathaniel Macon*, 19. The Macon-Eaton Bible, Southern Historical Collection, contains an entry giving the date of death as July 27.

78. Edwards, *Memoir of Nathaniel Macon*, 19-20. Edwards's credible account does raise some questions for a modern visitor to the gravesite. For instance, Macon's wife and son are buried next to him. Were they already there, and he joined them? Were they moved there later to join him? Would Macon have interred them in the same bleak ground he chose for himself? Dodd says that Hannah was buried not far from the dwelling (*Life of Nathaniel Macon*, 45). Both Thomas Pittman and Dodd say that Macon requested burial beside his wife (thus she was already on the current site), but neither cites a source. See Thomas M. Pittman, *Nathaniel Macon: An Address* (Greensboro, N.C.: Guilford Battle Ground Co., 1902), 16-18; Dodd, *Life of Nathaniel Macon*, 398-399. Edwards makes no mention of other graves on the "sterile ridge," and he implies that Macon chose the worthless ground with his lifelong disdain for memorialization.

When the enormous crowd gathered at Buck Spring in July heat to recall and celebrate the memory of Nathaniel Macon, many of them knew that a Revolutionary soldier and Old Republican was gone. Surely, some of them also sensed that the slow-paced world of the independent farmer that he and his friend Thomas Jefferson had prized was also fading. Banks with their paper money and credit were expanding throughout North Carolina as they were in the South and the nation. Steamboats plied the Roanoke and its engineered canals. As travelers to the burial of "the last of the Romans" rode to Buck Spring, many of them would have seen ties being laid for the Raleigh and Gaston Railroad. Amid the ample food and drink at the funeral did anyone taste the irony?

*   *   *

Two years before he died, Nathaniel Macon asserted his preference for the word "planter" over "farmer." It "conveyed to his mind more of independence and plenty." What did Macon mean?

The foremost requirement for the independence Macon referred to was ownership of land. "Farmer" to him implied "a state of tenantry," of leasing rather than owning. Born under British rule, fighting in the American Revolution, and participating in the formation of new governments, Macon was part of that generation of southerners who believed that ownership of land and freedom from debt afforded the independence and moral character essential to liberty. Self-sufficiency and avoidance of financial anxiety (including excessive taxes) fostered independence. When money rather than food, clothing, and shelter became the measure of wealth, the moral fabric of society suffered.[79] Throughout his long life, Macon avoided debt and paper money. If he was compelled to use currency, he sought to draw it from a state bank rather than any federal branch. Despite a long political career, he never solicited for any office, and although a lifelong Democrat, he deplored and eventually refused to participate in the caucus system that developed within his party. He never cloaked his political opinions in either subtlety or flattery but stated them plainly, consistently, and infrequently. As close as he was to Jefferson and Randolph and others in his time in Congress, more than once he struck an independent course from them politically when his principles dictated it.[80]

For example, Macon adamantly refused to have any image of himself made during his lifetime. See John Hill Wheeler, *Reminiscences and Memoirs of North Carolina and Eminent North Carolinians* (Columbus, Ohio: Columbus Printing Works, 1884), 454.

79. Kirk, *Randolph of Roanoke*, 85; Pauline Maier, "Early Revolutionary Leaders in the South and the Problem of Southern Distinctiveness" in *The Southern Experience in the American Revolution*, ed. Jeffrey J. Crow and Larry E. Tise (Chapel Hill: University of North Carolina Press, 1978), 15-18; Risjord, *Old Republicans*, 3; H. Watson, "Squire Oldway and His Friends," 115.

80. Nathaniel Macon to Weldon Edwards, December 24, 1827, March 3, 1828, Macon Papers; Benton, *Thirty Years' View*, 34-35; Edwards, *Memoir of Nathaniel Macon*, 11-14.

Macon, like Thomas Jefferson, cherished individual freedom and an economic ideal of agriculture pursued on independent farms. Jefferson, praising Macon's integrity, modest virtue, and political pragmatism, once called Macon "Ultimus Romanorum"—the last of the Romans. Pendleton's Lithography, "Thomas Jefferson, Third President of the United States," c. 1828. Engraving, after original painting by Gilbert Stuart, in American Memory Collections, Library of Congress, Washington, D.C.

The plenty that Macon most prized was that afforded by a self-sufficient freehold. Never as wealthy as the leading planters of the Roanoke Valley, he was still comfortably well-to-do.[81] His contemporaries uniformly referred to his warm hospitality. While Macon would grouse from time to time about market prices for crops or a bad harvest, he never alluded to having to borrow money to make it through a rough period, much less to speculate. The untimely deaths of his elder daughter and her husband in 1827 and 1828 burdened Macon with assisting in the care of their orphaned children. While that circumstance caused him much grief,

81. Censer, *North Carolina Planters*, xiv. For purposes of her study, Censer looks at planters owning seventy or more slaves in one county in the 1830 census. Macon just missed that definition in 1830 but had exceeded it by 1837, probably through natural increase rather than purchase.

On June 29, 1837, Macon died quietly at Buck Spring. The *Raleigh Register* reported that between one thousand and fifteen hundred whites and several hundred blacks attended Macon's funeral. He had selected a gravesite about three hundred yards east of his home because the land was "so barren no one will ever desire to cultivate it." He did not believe that good farmland should be devoted to the dead. He further directed that stones thrown up by plows working the land be used to cover his grave. Photograph of Macon's gravesite at Buck Spring by Michael Southern, courtesy of the State Archives.

he did not complain of financial distress.[82] If many Roanoke planters lived luxuriously, Macon was content but not ostentatious in his plenty.

Finally, it must be noted that Macon had no intention of defaming farmers when defining planters. To be sure, planters had *more* independence and plenty and less tenantry than farmers, but both were agrarians, close to the soil and away from the corruption of cities. Like Jefferson and Randolph, Macon valued farming the land above all other employment.[83] It was "truly faring well," as he had said in 1828.

＊   ＊   ＊

82. Edwards, *Memoir of Nathaniel Macon*, 13; John Randolph to Weldon Edwards, January 7, 1828, Edwards Papers.
83. Larson, "Jefferson's Union and the Problem of Internal Improvements," 343-345; Weaver, *The Southern Tradition at Bay*, 18.

The modern traveler to the gravesite of Nathaniel Macon sees what he would have rejected: a bronze plaque mounted on granite detailing his political accomplishments. The visitor no longer finds close at hand the large stones covering the graves of Macon, his wife, and son. No plows are turning over big rocks now near the barren ground Macon chose.

To comply with the old man's request that passersby throw a stone on his remains, the visitor can only toss a pebble from the sandy ground surrounding the site. Having turned off the state highway, the traveler has arrived by automobile over paved roads past the small, neat houses of white and black families—some with satellite dishes in their yards. The countryside for miles around is still farmed, and fox and deer still roam the thick woodlands. On certain days you can even hear the blare of a hunting horn calling hounds to the chase.

Index